I0749296

AULD LICHT IDYLS

J. M. BARRIE

Auld Licht Idyls

J. M. Barrie

PO Box 2211
Fairfield, IA 52556
www.1stworldlibrary.com
First Edition

LCCN: 2007920652

Softcover ISBN: 978-1-4218-3964-6
Hardcover ISBN: 978-1-4218-3864-9
eBook ISBN: 978-1-4218-4064-2

1st World Library Literary Society

Giving Back to the World

"If you want to work on the core problem, it's early school literacy."

- James Barksdale, former CEO of Netscape

"No skill is more crucial to the future of a child, or to a democratic and prosperous society, than literacy."

- Los Angeles Times

Literacy... means far more than learning how to read and write... The aim is to transmit... knowledge and promote social participation."

- UNESCO

"Literacy is not a luxury, it is a right and a responsibility. If our world is to meet the challenges of the twenty-first century we must harness the energy and creativity of all our citizens."

- President Bill Clinton

"Parents should be encouraged to read to their children, and teachers should be equipped with all available techniques for teaching literacy, so the varying needs and capacities of individual kids can be taken into account."

- Hugh Mackay

TO

FREDERICK GREENWOOD

CONTENTS

CHAPTER I

THE SCHOOL-HOUSE

Early this morning I opened a window in my school-house in the glen of Quharity, awakened by the shivering of a starving sparrow against the frosted glass. As the snowy sash creaked in my hand, he made off to the waterspout that suspends its "tangles" of ice over a gaping tank, and, rebounding from that, with a quiver of his little black breast, bobbed through the network of wire and joined a few of his fellows in a forlorn hop round the henhouse in search of food. Two days ago my hilarious bantam-cock, saucy to the last, my cheeriest companion, was found frozen in his own water-trough, the corn-saucer in three pieces by his side. Since then I have taken the hens into the house. At meal-times they litter the hearth with each other's feathers; but for the most part they give little trouble, roosting on the rafters of the low-roofed kitchen among staves and fishing-rods.

Another white blanket has been spread upon the glen since I looked out last night; for over the same wilderness of snow that has met my gaze for a week, I see the steading of Waster Lunny sunk deeper into the waste. The school-house, I suppose, serves similarly as a snow-mark for the people at the farm. Unless that is Waster Lunny's grieve foddering the cattle in the snow, not a living thing is visible. The ghostlike hills that pen in the glen have ceased to echo to the sharp crack of the sportsman's gun (so clear in the frosty air as to be a warning to every rabbit and partridge in the valley); and only giant Catlaw shows here and there a black ridge, rearing his head at the entrance to the glen and struggling ineffectually to cast off his shroud. Most wintry sign of all I think, as I close the window hastily, is the open farm-stile, its poles lying embedded in the snow where they were last flung by Waster Lunny's herd. Through the still air comes from a distance a vibration as of a tuning-fork: a robin, perhaps, alighting on the wire of a broken fence.

In the warm kitchen, where I dawdle over my breakfast, the widowed bantam-hen has perched on the back of my drowsy cat. It is needless to go through the form of opening the school to-day; for, with the exception of Waster Lunny's girl, I have had no scholars for nine days. Yesterday she announced that there would be no more schooling till it was fresh, "as she wasna comin';" and indeed, though the smoke from the farm chimneys is a pretty prospect for a snowed-up school-master, the trudge between the two houses must be weary work for a bairn. As for the other children, who have to come from all parts of the hills and glen, I may not see them for weeks. Last year the school was practically deserted for a month. A pleasant outlook, with the March examinations staring me in the face, and an inspector fresh from Oxford. I wonder what he would say if he saw me to-day digging myself out of the school-house with the spade I now keep for the purpose in my bedroom.

The kail grows brittle from the snow in my dank and cheerless garden. A crust of bread gathers timid pheasants round me. The robins, I see, have made the coal-house their home. Waster Lunny's dog never barks without rousing my sluggish cat to a joyful response. It is Dutch courage with the birds and beasts of the glen, hard driven for food; but I look attentively for them in these long forenoons, and they have begun to regard me as one of themselves. My breath freezes, despite my pipe, as I peer from the door: and with a fortnight-old newspaper I retire to the ingle-nook. The friendliest thing I have seen to-day is the well-smoked ham suspended, from my kitchen rafters. It was a gift from the farm of Tullin, with a load of peats, the day before the snow began to fall. I doubt if I have seen a cart since.

This afternoon I was the not altogether passive spectator of a curious scene in natural history. My feet encased in stout "tackety" boots, I had waded down two of Waster Lunny's fields to the glen burn: in summer the never-failing larder from which, with wriggling worm or garish fly, I can any morning whip a savory breakfast; in the winter time the only thing in the valley that defies the ice-king's chloroform. I watched the water twisting black and solemn through the snow, the ragged ice on its edge proof of the toughness of the struggle with the frost, from which it has, after all, crept only half victorious. A bare wild rose-bush on the farther bank was violently agitated, and then there ran from its root a black-headed rat with wings. Such was the general effect. I was not less interested when my startled eyes divided this phenomenon into its component parts, and recognized in the disturbance on the opposite bank only another fierce struggle among the hungry animals for existence: they need no professor to teach them the doctrine of the survival of the fittest. A weasel had gripped a water-hen (whit-tit and beltie they are called In these parts) cowering at the root of the rose-bush, and was being dragged down the bank by the terrified bird, which made for the water as its only chance of escape. In less disadvantageous circumstances the weasel would have made short work of his victim; but as he only had the bird by the tail, the prospects of the combatants were equalized. It was the tug-of-war being played with a life as the stakes. "If I do not reach the water," was the argument that went on in the heaving little breast of the one, "I am a dead bird." "If this water-hen," reasoned the other, "reaches the burn, my supper vanishes with her." Down the sloping bank the hen had distinctly the best of it, but after that came a yard, of level snow, and here she tugged and screamed in vain. I had so far been an unobserved spectator; but my sympathies were with the beltie, and, thinking it high time to interfere, I jumped into the water. The water-hen gave one mighty final tug and toppled into the burn; while the weasel viciously showed me his teeth, and then stole slowly up the bank to the rose-bush, whence, "girning," he watched me lift his exhausted victim from the water, and set off with her for the school-house. Except for her draggled tail, she already looks wonderfully composed, and so long as the frost holds I shall have little difficulty in keeping her with me. On Sunday I found a frozen sparrow, whose heart had almost ceased to beat, in the disused pigsty, and put him for warmth into my breast-pocket. The ungrateful little scrub bolted without a word of thanks about ten minutes afterward, to the alarm of my cat, which had not known his whereabouts.

I am alone in the school-house. On just such an evening as this last year my desolation drove me to Waster Lunny, where I was storm-stayed for the night. The recollection decides me to court my own warm hearth, to challenge my right hand again to a game at the "dambrod" against my left. I do not lock the school-house door at nights; for even a highwayman (there is no such luck) would be received with open arms, and I doubt if there be a barred door in all the glen. But it is cosier to put on the shutters. The road to Thrums has lost itself miles down the valley. I wonder what they are doing out in the world. Though I am the Free Church precentor in Thrums (ten pounds a year, and the little town is five miles away), they have not seen me for three weeks. A packman whom I thawed yesterday at my kitchen fire tells me that last Sabbath only the Auld Lichts held service. Other people realized that they were snowed up. Far up the glen, after it twists out of view, a manse and half a dozen thatched cottages that are there may still show a candle-light, and the crumbling gravestones keep cold vigil round the gray old kirk. Heavy shadows fade into the sky to the north. A flake trembles against the window; but it is too cold for much snow to-night. The shutter bars the outer world from the school-house.

CHAPTER II

THRUMS

Thrums is the name I give here to the handful of houses jumbled together in a cup, which is the town nearest the school-house. Until twenty years ago its every other room, earthen-floored and showing the rafters overhead, had a hand-loom, and hundreds of weavers lived and died Thoreaus "ben the hoose" without knowing it. In those days the cup overflowed and left several houses on the top of the hill, where their cold skeletons still stand. The road that climbs from the square, which is Thrums' heart, to the north is so steep and straight, that in a sharp frost children hunker at the top and are blown down with a roar and a rush on rails of ice. At such times, when viewed from the cemetery where the traveller from the school-house gets his first glimpse of the little town. Thrums is but two church-steeples and a dozen red-stone patches standing out of a snow-heap. One of the steeples belongs to the new Free Kirk, and the other to the parish church, both of which the first Auld Licht minister I knew ran past when he had not time to avoid them by taking a back wynd. He was but a pocket edition of a man, who grew two inches after he was called; but he was so full of the cure of souls, that he usually scudded to it with his coat-tails quarrelling behind him. His successor, whom I knew better, was a greater scholar, and said, "Let us see what this is in the original Greek," as an ordinary man might invite a friend to dinner; but he never wrestled as Mr. Dishart, his successor, did with the pulpit cushions, nor flung himself at the pulpit door.

Nor was he so "hard on the Book," as Lang Tammas, the precentor, expressed it, meaning that he did not bang the Bible with his fist as much as might have been wished.

Thrums had been known to me for years before I succeeded the captious dominie at the school-house in the glen. The dear old soul who originally induced me to enter the Auld Licht kirk by lamenting the "want of Christ" in the minister's discourses was my first landlady. For the last ten years of her life she was bedridden, and only her interest in the kirk kept her alive. Her case against the minister was that he did not call to denounce her sufficiently often for her sins, her pleasure being to hear him bewailing her on his knees as one who was probably past praying for. She was as sweet and pure a woman as I ever knew, and had her wishes been horses, she would have sold them and kept (and looked after) a minister herself.

There are few Auld Licht communities in Scotland nowadays —perhaps because people are now so well off, for the most devout Auld Lichts were always poor, and their last years were generally a grim struggle with the workhouse. Many a heavy-eyed, back-bent weaver has won his Waterloo in Thrums fighting on his stumps. There are a score or two of them left still, for, though there are now two factories in the town, the clatter of the hand-loom can yet be heard, and they have been starving themselves of late until they have saved up enough money to get another minister.

The square is packed away in the centre of Thrums, and irregularly built little houses squeeze close to it like chickens clustering round a hen. Once the Auld Lichts held property in the square, but other denominations have bought them out of it, and now few of them are even to be found in the main streets that make for the rim of the cup. They live in the kirk wynd, or in retiring little houses, the builder of which does not seem to have remembered that it is a good plan to have a road leading to houses until after they were finished. Narrow paths straggling round gardens, some of them with stunted gates, which it is commoner to step over than, to open, have been formed to reach these dwellings, but in winter they are running streams, and then the best way to reach a house such as that of Tammy Mealmaker the wright, pronounced wiricht, is over a broken dyke and a pig-sty. Tammy, who died a bachelor, had been soured in his youth by a disappointment in love, of which he spoke but seldom. She lived far away in a town which he had wandered in the days when his blood ran hot, and they became engaged. Unfortunately, however, Tammy forgot her name, and he never knew the address; so there the affair ended, to his silent grief. He admitted himself, over his snuff-mull of an evening, that he was a very ordinary character, but a certain halo of horror was cast over the whole family by their connection with little Joey Sutie, who was pointed at in Thrums as the laddie that whistled when he went past the minister. Joey became a pedler, and was found dead one raw morning dangling over a high wall within a few miles of Thrums. When climbing the dyke his pack had slipped back, the strap round his neck, and choked him.

You could generally tell an Auld Licht in Thrums when you passed him, his dull, vacant face wrinkled over a heavy wob. He wore tags of yarn round his trousers beneath the knee, that looked like ostentatious garters, and frequently his jacket of corduroy was put on beneath his waistcoat. If he was too old to carry his load on his back, he wheeled it on a creaking barrow, and when he met a friend they said, "Ay, Jeames," and "Ay, Davit," and then could think of nothing else. At long intervals they passed through the square, disappearing or coming into sight round the town-house which stands on the south side of it, and guards the entrance to a steep brae that leads down and then twists up on its lonely way to the county town. I like to linger over the square, for it was from an upper window in it that I got to know Thrums. On Saturday nights, when the Auld Licht young men came into the square dressed and washed to look at the young women errand-going, and to laugh some time afterward to each other, it presented a glare of light; and here even came the cheap jacks and the Fair Circassian, and the showman, who, besides playing "The Mountain Maid and the Shepherd's Bride," exhibited part of the tall of Balaam's ass, the helm of Noah's ark, and the tartan plaid in which Flora McDonald wrapped Prince Charlie. More select entertainment, such as Shuffle Kitty's wax-work, whose motto was, "A rag to pay, and in you go," were given in a hall whose approach was by an outside stair. On the Muckle Friday, the fair for which children storing their pocket-money would accumulate sevenpence halfpenny in less than six months, the square was crammed with gingerbread stalls, bagpipers, fiddlers, and monstrosities who were gifted with second-sight. There was a bearded man, who had neither legs nor arms, and was drawn through the streets in a small cart by four dogs. By looking at you he could see all the clock-work inside, as could a boy who was led about by his mother at the end of a string. Every Friday there was the market, when a dozen ramshackle carts containing vegetables and cheap crockery filled the centre of the square, resting in line on their shafts. A score of farmers' wives or daughters in old-world garments squatted against the town-house within walls of butter on cabbage-leaves, eggs and chickens. Toward evening the voice of the buckie-man shook the square, and rival fish-cadgers, terrible characters who ran races on horseback, screamed libels at each other over a fruiterer's barrow. Then it was time for douce Auld Lichts to go home, draw their stools near the fire, spread their red handkerchiefs over their legs to prevent their trousers getting singed, and read their "Pilgrim's Progress."

In my school-house, however, I seem to see the square most readily in the Scotch mist which so often filled it, loosening the stones and choking the drains. There was then no rattle of rain against my window-sill, nor dancing of diamond drops on the roofs, but blobs of water grew on the panes of glass to reel heavily down them. Then the sodden square would have shed abundant tears if you could have taken it in your hands and wrung it like a dripping cloth. At such a time the square would be empty but for one vegetable-cart left in the care of a lean collie, which, tied to the wheel, whined and shivered underneath. Pools of water gather in the coarse sacks that have been spread over the potatoes and bundles of greens, which turn to manure in their lidless barrels. The eyes of the whimpering dog never leave a black close over which hangs the sign of the Bull, probably the refuge of the hawker. At long intervals a farmer's gig rumbles over the bumpy, ill-paved square, or a native, with his head buried in his coat, peeps out of doors, skurries across the way, and vanishes. Most of the leading shops are here, and the decorous draper ventures a few yards from the pavement to scan the sky, or note the effect of his new arrangement in scarves. Planted against his door is the butcher, Henders Todd, white-aproned, and with a knife in his hand, gazing interestedly at the draper, for a mere man may look at an elder. The tinsmith brings out his steps, and, mounting them, stealthily removes the saucepans and pepper-pots that dangle on a wire above his sign-board. Pulling to his door he shuts out the foggy light that showed in his solder-strewn workshop. The square is deserted again. A bundle of sloppy parsley slips from the hawker's cart and topples over the wheel in driblets. The puddles in the sacks overflow and run together. The dog has twisted his chain round a barrel and yelps sharply. As if in response comes a rush of other dogs. A terrified fox-terrier tears across the square with half a score of mongrels, the butcher's mastiff, and some collies at his heels; he is doubtless a stranger, who has insulted them by his glossy coat. For two seconds the square shakes to an invasion of dogs, and then again there is only one dog in sight.

No one will admit the Scotch mist. It "looks saft." The tinsmith "wudna wonder but what it was makkin' for rain." Tammas Haggart and Pete Lunan dander into sight bareheaded, and have to stretch out their hands to discover what the weather is like. By-and-bye they come to a standstill to discuss the immortality of the soul, and then they are looking silently at the Bull. Neither speaks, but they begin to move toward the inn at the same time, and its door closes on them before they know what they are doing. A few minutes afterward Jinny Dundas, who is Pete's wife, runs straight for the Bull in her short gown, which is tucked up very high, and emerges with her husband soon afterward. Jinny is voluble, but Pete says nothing. Tammas follows later, putting his head out at the door first, and looking cautiously about him to see if any one is in sight. Pete is a U.P., and may be left to his fate, but the Auld Licht minister thinks that, though it be hard work, Tammas is worth saving.

To the Auld Licht of the past there were three degrees of damnation—auld kirk, playacting, chapel. Chapel was the name always given to the English Church, of which I am too much an Auld Licht myself to care to write even now. To belong to the chapel was, in Thrums, to be a Roman Catholic, and the boy who flung a clod of earth at the English minister —who called the Sabbath Sunday—or dropped a "divet" down his chimney was held to be in the right way. The only pleasant story Thrums could tell of the chapel was that its steeple once fell. It is surprising that an English church was ever suffered to be built in such a place; though probably the county gentry had something to do with it. They travelled about too much to be good men. Small though Thrums used to be, it had four kirks in all before the disruption, and then another, which split into two immediately afterward. The spire of the parish church, known as the auld kirk, commands a view of the square, from which the entrance to the kirk-yard would be visible, if it were not hidden by the town-house. The kirk-yard has long been crammed, and is not now in use, but the church is sufficiently large to hold nearly all the congregations in Thrums. Just at the gate lived Pete Todd, the father of Sam'l, a man of whom the Auld Lichts had reason to be proud. Pete was an every-day man at ordinary times, and was even said, when his wife, who had been long ill, died, to have clasped his hands and exclaimed, "Hip, hip, hurrah!" adding only as an afterthought, "The Lord's will be done." But midsummer was his great opportunity. Then took place the rouping of the seats in the parish church. The scene was the kirk itself, and the seats being put up to auction were knocked down to the highest bidder. This sometimes led to the breaking of the peace. Every person was present who was at all particular as to where he sat, and an auctioneer was engaged for the day. He rouped the kirk-seats like potato-drills, beginning by asking for a bid. Every seat was put up to auction separately; for some were much more run after than others, and the men were instructed by their wives what to bid for. Often the women joined in, and as they bid excitedly against each other the church rang with opprobrious epithets. A man would come to the roup late, and learn that the seat he wanted had been knocked down. He maintained that he had been unfairly treated, or denounced the local laird to whom the seat-rents went. If he did not get the seat he would leave the kirk. Then the woman who had forestalled him wanted to know what he meant by glaring at her so, and the auction was interrupted. Another member would "thrip down the throat" of the auctioneer that he had a right to his former seat if he continued to pay the same price for it. The auctioneer was screamed at for favoring his friends, and at times the group became so noisy that men and women had to be forcibly ejected. Then was Pete's chance. Hovering at the gate, he caught the angry people on their way home and took them into his workshop by an outside stair. There he assisted them in denouncing the parish kirk, with the view of getting them to forswear it. Pete made a good many Auld Lichts in his time out of unpromising material.

Sights were to be witnessed in the parish church at times that could not have been made more impressive by the Auld Lichts themselves. Here sinful women were grimly taken to task by the minister, who, having thundered for a time against adultery in general, called upon one sinner in particular to stand forth. She had to step forward into a pew near the pulpit, where, alone and friendless, and stared at by the congregation, she cowered in tears beneath his denunciations. In that seat she had to remain during the forenoon service. She returned home alone, and had to come back alone to her solitary seat in the afternoon. All day no one dared speak to her. She was as much an object of contumely as the thieves and smugglers who, in the end of last century, it was the privilege of Feudal Bailie Wood (as he was called) to whip round the square.

It is nearly twenty years since the gardeners had their last "walk" in Thrums, and they survived all the other benefit societies that walked once every summer. There was a "weavers' walk" and five or six others, the "women's walk" being the most picturesque. These were processions of the members of benefit societies through the square and wynds, and all the women walked in white, to the number of a hundred or more, behind the Tillie-drum band, Thrums having in those days no band of its own.

From the northwest corner of the square a narrow street sets off, jerking this way and that, as if uncertain what point to make for. Here lurks the post-office, which had once the reputation of being as crooked in its ways as the street itself.

A railway line runs into Thrums now. The sensational days of the post-office were when the letters were conveyed officially in a creaking old cart from Tilliedrum. The "pony" had seen better days than the cart, and always looked as if he were just on the point of succeeding in running away from it. Hooky Crewe was driver—so called because an iron hook was his substitute for a right arm. Robbie Proctor, the blacksmith, made the hook and fixed it in. Crewe suffered from rheumatism, and when he felt it coming on he stayed at home. Sometimes his cart came undone in a snow-drift; when Hooky, extricated from the fragments by some chance wayfarer, was deposited with his mail-bag (of which he always kept a grip by the hook) in a farmhouse. It was his boast that his letters always reached their destination eventually. They might be a long time about it, but "slow *and* sure" was his motto. Hooky emphasized his "slow *and* sure" by taking a snuff. He was a godsend to the postmistress, for to his failings or the infirmities of his gig were charged all delays.

At the time I write of, the posting of the letter took as long and was as serious an undertaking as the writing. That means a good deal, for many of the letters were written to dictation by the Thrums school-master, Mr. Fleemister, who belonged to the Auld Kirk. He was one of the few persons in the community who looked upon the despatch of his letters by the post-mistress as his right, and not a favor on her part; there was a long-standing feud between them accordingly. After a few tumblers of Widow Stables' treacle-beer—in the concoction of which she was the acknowledged mistress for miles around—the schoolmaster would sometimes go the length of hinting that he could get the post-mistress dismissed any day. This mighty power seemed to rest on a knowledge of "steamed" letters. Thrums had a high respect for the school-master; but among themselves the weavers agreed that, even if he did write to the Government, Lizzie Harrison, the post-mistress, would refuse to transmit the letter. The more shrewd ones among us kept friends with both parties; for, unless you could write "writ-hand," you could not compose a letter without the school-master's assistance; and, unless Lizzie was so courteous as to send it to its destination, it might lie—or so it was thought—much too long in the box. A letter addressed by the schoolmaster found great disfavor in Lizzie's eyes. You might explain to her that you had merely called in his assistance because you were a poor hand at writing yourself, but that was held no excuse. Some addressed their own envelopes with much labor, and sought to palm off the whole as their handiwork. It reflects on the post-mistress somewhat that she had generally found them out by next day, when, if in a specially vixenish mood, she did not hesitate to upbraid them for their perfidy.

To post a letter you did not merely saunter to the post-office and drop it into the box. The cautious correspondent first went into the shop and explained to Lizzie how matters stood. She kept what she called a bookseller's shop as well as the post-office; but the supply of books corresponded exactly to the lack of demand for them, and her chief trade was in nick-nacks, from marbles and money-boxes up to concertinas. If he found the post-mistress in an amiable mood, which was only now and then, the caller led up craftily to the object of his visit. Having discussed the weather and the potato-disease, he explained that his sister Mary, whom Lizzie would remember, had married a fishmonger in Dundee. The fishmonger had lately started on himself and was doing well. They had four children. The youngest had had a severe attack of measles. No news had been got of Mary for twelve months; and Annie, his other sister, who lived in Thrums, had been at him of late for not writing. So he had written a few lines; and, in fact, he had the letter with him. The letter was then produced, and examined by the postmistress. If the address was in the schoolmaster's handwriting, she professed her inability to read it. Was this a *t* or an *l* or an *i?* was that a *b* or a *d?* This was a cruel revenge on Lizzie's part; for the sender of the letter was completely at her mercy. The school-master's name being tabooed in her presence, he was unable to explain that the writing was not his own; and as for deciding between the *t*'s and *l*'s, he could not do it. Eventually he would be directed to put the letter into the box. They would do their best with it, Lizzie said, but in a voice that suggested how little hope she had of her efforts to decipher it proving successful.

There was an opinion among some of the people that the letter should not be stamped by the sender. The proper thing to do was to drop a penny for the stamp into the box along with the letter, and then Lizzie would see that it was all right. Lizzie's acquaintance with the handwriting of every person in the place who could write gave her a great advantage. You would perhaps drop into her shop some day to make a purchase, when she would calmly produce a letter you had posted several days before. In explanation she would tell you that you had not put a stamp on it, or that she suspected there was money in it, or that you had addressed it to the wrong place. I remember an old man, a relative of my own, who happened for once in his life to have several letters to post at one time. The circumstance was so out of the common that he considered it only reasonable to make Lizzie a small present.

Perhaps the post-mistress was belied; but if she did not "steam" the letters and confide their titbits to favored friends of her own sex, it is difficult to see how all the gossip got out. The school-master once played an unmanly trick on her, with the view of catching her in the act. He was a bachelor who had long been given up by all the maids in the town. One day, however, he wrote a letter to an imaginary lady in the county-town, asking her to be his, and going into full particulars about his income, his age, and his prospects. A male friend in the secret, at the other end, was to reply, in a lady's handwriting, accepting him, and also giving personal particulars. The first letter was written; and an answer arrived in due course—two days, the school-master said, after date. No other person knew of this scheme for the undoing of the post-mistress, yet in a very short time the school-master's coming marriage was the talk of Thrums. Everybody became suddenly aware of the lady's name, of her abode, and of the sum of money she was to bring her husband. It was even noised abroad that the school-master had represented his age as a good ten years less than it was. Then the school-master divulged everything. To his mortification, he was not quite believed. All the proof he could bring forward to support his story was this: that time would show whether he got married or not. Foolish man! this argument was met by another, which was accepted at once. The lady had jilted the school-master. Whether this explanation came from the post-office, who shall say? But so long as he lived the school-master was twitted about the lady who threw him over. He took his revenge in two ways. He wrote and posted letters exceedingly abusive of the post-mistress. The matter might be libellous; but then, as he pointed out, she would incriminate herself if she "brought him up" about it. Probably Lizzie felt his other insult more. By publishing his suspicions of her on every possible occasion he got a few people to seal their letters. So bitter was his feeling against her that he was even willing to supply the wax.

They know all about post-offices in Thrums now, and even jeer at the telegraph-boy's uniform. In the old days they gathered round him when he was seen in the street, and escorted him to his destination in triumph. That, too, was after Lizzie had gone the way of all the earth. But perhaps they are not even yet as knowing as they think themselves. I was told the other day that one of them took out a postal order, meaning to send the money to a relative, and kept the order as a receipt.

I have said that the town is sometimes full of snow. One frosty Saturday, seven years ago, I trudged into it from the school-house, and on the Monday morning we could not see Thrums anywhere.

I was in one of the proud two-storied houses in the place, and could have shaken hands with my friends without from the upper windows. To get out of doors you had to walk upstairs. The outlook was a sea of snow fading into white hills and sky, with the quarry standing out red and ragged to the right like a rock in the ocean. The Auld Licht manse was gone, but had left its garden-trees behind, their lean branches soft with snow. Roofs were humps in the white blanket. The spire of the Established Kirk stood up cold and stiff, like a monument to the buried inhabitants.

Those of the natives who had taken the precaution of conveying spades into their houses the night before, which is my plan at the school-house, dug themselves out. They hobbled cautiously over the snow, sometimes sinking into it to their knees, when they stood still and slowly took in the situation. It had been snowing more or less for a week, but in a commonplace kind of way, and they had gone to bed thinking all was well. This night the snow must have fallen as if the heavens had opened up, determined to shake themselves free of it for ever.

The man who first came to himself and saw what was to be done was young Henders Ramsay. Henders had no fixed occupation, being but an "orra man" about the place, and the best thing known of him is that his mother's sister was a Baptist. He feared God, man, nor the minister; and all the learning he had was obtained from assiduous study of a grocer's window. But for one brief day he had things his own way in the town, or, speaking strictly, on the top of it. With a spade, a broom, and a pickaxe, which sat lightly on his broad shoulders (he was not even back-bent, and that showed him no respectable weaver), Henders delved his way to the nearest house, which formed one of a row, and addressed the inmates down the chimney. They had already been clearing it at the other end, or his words would have been choked. "You're snawed up, Davit," cried Henders, in a voice that was entirely business-like; "hae ye a spade?" A conversation ensued up and down this unusual channel of communication. The unlucky householder, taking no thought of the morrow, was without a spade. But if Henders would clear away the snow from his door he would be "varra obleeged." Henders, however, had to come to terms first. "The chairge is saxpence, Davit," he shouted. Then a haggling ensued. Henders must be neighborly. A plate of broth, now—or, say, twopence. But Henders was obdurate. "I'se nae time to argy-bargy wi' ye, Davit. Gin ye're no willin' to say saxpence, I'm aff to Will'um Pyatt's. He's buried too." So the victim had to make up his mind to one of two things: he must either say saxpence or remain where he was.

If Henders was "promised," he took good care that no snowed-up inhabitant should perjure himself. He made his way to a window first, and, clearing the snow from the top of it, pointed out that he could not conscientiously proceed further until the debt had been paid. "Money doon," he cried, as soon as he reached a pane of glass; or, "Come awa wi' my saxpence noo."

The belief that this day had not come to Henders unexpectedly was borne out by the method of the crafty callant. His charges varied from sixpence to half-a-crown, according to the wealth and status of his victims; and when, later on, there were rivals in the snow, he had the discrimination to reduce his minimum fee to threepence. He had the honor of digging out three ministers at one shilling, one and threepence, and two shillings respectively.

Half a dozen times within the next fortnight the town was re-buried in snow. This generally happened in the night-time; but the inhabitants were not to be caught unprepared again. Spades stood ready to their hands in the morning, and they fought their way above ground without Henders Ramsay's assistance. To clear the snow from the narrow wynds and pends, however, was a task not to be attempted; and the Auld Lichts, at least, rested content when enough light got into their workshops to let them see where their looms stood. Wading through beds of snow they did not much mind; but they wondered what would happen to their houses when the thaw came.

The thaw was slow in coming. Snow during the night and several degrees of frost by day were what Thrums began to accept as a revised order of nature. Vainly the Thrums doctor, whose practice extends into the glens, made repeated attempts to reach his distant patients, twice driving so far into the dreary waste that he could neither go on nor turn back. A ploughman who contrived to gallop ten miles for him did not get home for a week. Between the town, which is nowadays an agricultural centre of some importance, and the outlying farms communication was cut off for a month; and I heard subsequently of one farmer who did not see a human being, unconnected with his own farm, for seven weeks. The school-house, which I managed to reach only two days behind time, was closed for a fortnight, and even in Thrums there was only a sprinkling of scholars.

On Sundays the feeling between the different denominations ran high, and the middling good folk who did not go to church counted those who did. In the Established Church there was a sparse gathering, who waited in vain for the minister. After a time it got abroad that a flag of distress was flying from the manse, and then they saw that the minister was storm-stayed. An office-bearer offered to conduct service; but the others present thought they had done their duty and went home. The U.P. bell did not ring at all, and the kirk-gates were not opened. The Free Kirk did bravely, however. The attendance in the forenoon amounted to seven, including the minister; but in the afternoon there was a turn-out of upward of fifty. How much denominational competition had to do with this, none can say; but the general opinion was that this muster to afternoon service was a piece of vainglory. Next

Sunday all the kirks were on their mettle, and, though the snow was drifting the whole day, services were general. It was felt that after the action of the Free Kirk the Established and the U.P.'s must show what they too were capable of. So, when, the bells rang-at eleven o'clock and two, church-goers began to pour out of every close. If I remember aright, the victory lay with, the U.P.'s by two women and a boy. Of course the Auld Lichts mustered in as great force as ever. The other kirks never dreamed of competing with them. What was regarded as a judgment on the Free Kirk for its boastfulness of spirit on the preceding Sunday happened during the forenoon. While the service was taking place a huge clod of snow slipped from the roof and fell right against the church door. It was some time before the prisoners could make up their minds to leave by the windows. What the Auld Lichts would have done in a similar predicament I cannot even conjecture.

That was the first warning of the thaw. It froze again; there was more snow; the thaw began in earnest; and then the streets were a sight to see. There was no traffic to turn the snow to slush, and, where it had not been piled up in walls a few feet from the houses, it remained in the narrow ways till it became a lake. It tried to escape through doorways, when it sank, slowly into the floors. Gentle breezes created a ripple on its surface, and strong winds lifted it into the air and flung it against the houses. It undermined the heaps of clotted snow till they tottered like icebergs and fell to pieces. Men made their way through, it on stilts. Had a frost followed, the result would have been appalling; but there was no more frost that winter. A fortnight passed before the place looked itself again, and even then congealed snow stood doggedly in the streets, while the country roads were like newly ploughed fields after rain. The heat from large fires soon penetrated through roofs of slate and thatch; and it was quite a common thing for a man to be flattened to the ground by a slithering of snow from above just as he opened his door. But it had seldom more than ten feet to fall. Most interesting of all was the novel sensation experienced as Thrums began to assume its familiar aspect, and objects so long buried that they had been half forgotten came back to view and use.

Storm-stead shows used to emphasize the severity of a Thrums winter. As the name indicates, these were gatherings of travelling booths in the winter-time. Half a century ago the country was overrun by itinerant showmen, who went their different ways in summer, but formed little colonies in the cold weather, when they pitched their tents in any empty field or disused quarry, and huddled together for the sake of warmth, not that they got much of it. Not more than five winters ago we had a storm-stead show on a small scale; but nowadays the farmers are less willing to give these wanderers a camping-place, and the people are less easily drawn to the entertainments provided, by fife and drum. The colony hung together until it was starved out, when it trailed itself elsewhere. I have often seen it forming. The first arrival would be what was popularly known as "Sam'l Mann's Tumbling-Booth," with its tumblers, jugglers, sword-swallowers, and balancers. This travelling show visited us regularly twice a year: once in summer for the Muckle Friday, when the performers were gay and stout, and even the horses had flesh on their bones; and again in the "back-end" of the year, when cold and hunger had taken the blood from their faces, and the scraggy dogs that whined at their side were lashed for licking the paint off the caravans. While the storm-stead show was in the vicinity the villages suffered from an invasion of these dogs. Nothing told more truly the dreadful tale of the showman's life in winter. Sam'l Mann's was a big show, and half a dozen smaller ones, most of which were familiar to us, crawled in its wake. Others heard of its whereabouts and came in from distant parts. There was the well-known Gubbins with his "A' the World in a Box," a halfpenny peep-show, in which all the world was represented by Joseph and his Brethren (with pit and coat), the bombardment of Copenhagen, the Battle of the Nile, Daniel in the Den of Lions, and Mount Etna in eruption. "Aunty Maggy's Whirligig" could be enjoyed on payment of an old pair of boots, a collection of rags, or the like. Besides these and other shows, there were the wandering minstrels, most of whom were "Waterloo veterans" wanting arms or a leg. I remember one whose arms had been "smashed by a thunderbolt at Jamaica." Queer, bent old dames, who superintended "lucky bags" or told fortunes, supplied the uncanny element, but hesitated to call themselves witches, for there can still be seen near Thrums the pool where these unfortunates used to be drowned, and in the session book of the Glen Quharity kirk can be read an old minute announcing that on a certain Sabbath there was no preaching because "the minister was away at the burning of a witch." To the storm-stead shows came the gypsies in great numbers. Claypots (which is a corruption of Claypits) was their headquarters near Thrums, and it is still sacred to their memory. It was a clachan of miserable little huts built entirely of clay from the dreary and sticky pit in which they had been flung together. A shapeless hole on one side was the doorway, and a little hole, stuffed with straw in winter, the window. Some of the remnants of these hovels still stand. Their occupants, though they went by the name of gypsies among themselves, were known to the weavers as the Claypots beggars; and their King was Jimmy Pawse. His regal dignity gave Jimmy the right to seek alms first when he chose to do so; thus he got the cream of a place before his subjects set to work. He was rather foppish in his dress; generally affecting a suit of gray cloth with showy metal buttons on it, and a broad blue bonnet. His wife was a little body like himself; and when they went a-begging, Jimmy with a meal-bag for alms on his back, she always took her husband's arm. Jimmy was the legal adviser of his subjects; his decision was considered final on all questions, and he guided them in their courtships as well as on their death-beds. He christened their children and officiated at their weddings, marrying them over the tongs.

The storm-stead show attracted old and young—to looking on from the outside. In the day-time the wagons and tents presented a dreary appearance, sunk in snow, the dogs shivering between the wheels, and but little other sign of life visible. When dusk came the lights were lit, and the drummer and fifer from the booth of tumblers were sent into the town to entice an audience. They marched quickly through, the nipping, windy streets, and then returned with two or three score of men, women, and children, plunging through the snow or mud at their heavy heels. It was Orpheus fallen from his high estate. What a mockery the glare of the lamps and the capers of the mountebanks were, and how satisfied were we to enjoy it all without going inside. I hear the "Waterloo veterans" still, and remember their patriotic outbursts:

> On the sixteenth day of June, brave boys, while cannon loud did roar,
> We being short of cavalry they pressed on us full sore;
> But British steel soon made them yield, though our numbers was but few,
> And death or victory was the word on the plains of Waterloo.

The storm-stead shows often found it easier to sink to rest in a field than to leave it. For weeks at a time they were snowed up, sufficiently to prevent any one from Thrums going near them, though not sufficiently to keep the pallid mummers indoors. That would in many cases have meant starvation. They managed to fight their way through storm and snowdrift to the high road and thence to the town, where they got meal and sometimes broth. The tumblers and jugglers used occasionally to hire an out-house in the town at these times—you may be sure they did not pay for it in advance—and give performances there. It is a curious thing, but true, that our herd-boys and others were sometimes struck with the stage-fever. Thrums lost boys to the show-men even in winter.

On the whole, the farmers and the people generally were wonderfully long-suffering with these wanderers, who I believe were more honest than was to be expected. They stole, certainly; but seldom did they steal anything more valuable than turnips. Sam'l Mann himself flushed proudly over the effect his show once had on an irate farmer. The farmer appeared in the encampment, whip in hand and furious. They must get off his land before nightfall. The crafty showman, however, prevailed upon him to take a look at the acrobats, and he enjoyed the performance so much that he offered to let them stay until the end of the week. Before that time came there was such a fall of snow that departure was out of the question; and it is to the farmer's credit that he sent Sam'l a bag of meal to tide him and his actors over the storm.

There were times when the showmen made a tour of the bothies, where they slung their poles and ropes and gave their poor performances to audiences that were not critical. The bothy being strictly the "man's" castle, the farmer never interfered; indeed, he was sometimes glad to see the show. Every other weaver in Thrums used to have a son a ploughman, and it was the men from the bothies who filled the square on the muckly. "Hands" are not huddled together nowadays in squalid barns more like cattle than men and women, but bothies in the neighborhood of Thrums are not yet things of the past. Many a ploughman delves his way to and from them still in all weathers, when the snow is on the ground; at the time of "hairst," and when the turnip "shaws" have just forced themselves through the earth, looking like straight rows of green needles. Here is a picture of a bothy of to-day that I visited recently. Over the door there is a waterspout that has given way, and as I entered I got a rush of rain down my neck. The passage was so small that one could easily have stepped from the doorway on to the ladder standing against the wall, which was there in lieu of a staircase. "Upstairs" was a mere garret, where a man could not stand erect even in the centre. It was entered by a square hole in the ceiling, at present closed by a clap-door in no way dissimilar to the trap-doors on a theatre stage. I climbed into this garret, which is at present used as a store-room for agricultural odds and ends. At harvest-time, however, it is inhabited—full to overflowing. A few decades ago as many as fifty laborers engaged for the harvest had to be housed in the farm out-houses on beds of straw. There was no help for it, and men and women had to congregate in these barns together. Up as early as five in the morning, they were generally dead tired by night; and, miserable though this system of herding them together was, they took it like stoics, and their very number served as a moral safeguard. Nowadays the harvest is gathered in so quickly, and machinery does so much that used to be done by hand, that this crowding of laborers together, which was the bothy system at its worst, is nothing like what it was. As many as six or eight men, however, are put up in the garret referred to during "hairst"-time, and the female laborers have to make the best of it in the barn. There is no doubt that on many farms the two sexes have still at this busy time to herd together even at night.

The bothy was but scantily furnished, though it consisted of two rooms. In the one, which was used almost solely as a sleeping apartment, there was no furniture to speak of, beyond two closet beds, and its bumpy earthen floor gave it a cheerless look. The other, which had a single bed, was floored with wood. It was not badly lit by two very small windows that faced each other, and, besides several stools, there was a long form against one of the walls. A bright fire of peat and coal—nothing in the world makes such a cheerful red fire as this combination—burned beneath a big kettle ("boiler" they called it), and there was a "press" or cupboard containing a fair assortment of cooking utensils. Of these some belonged to the bothy, while others were the private property of the tenants. A tin "pan" and "pitcher" of water stood near the door, and the table in the middle of the room was covered with oilcloth.

Four men and a boy inhabited this bothy, and the rain had driven them all indoors. In better weather they spend the leisure of the evening at the game of quoits, which is the standard pastime among Scottish ploughmen. They fish the neighboring streams, too, and have burn-trout for supper several times a week. When I entered, two of them were sitting by the fire playing draughts, or, as they called it, "the dam-brod." The dam-brod is the Scottish laborer's billiards; and he often attains to a remarkable proficiency at the game. Wylie, the champion draught-player, was once a herd-boy; and wonderful stories are current in all bothies of the times when his master called him into the farm-parlor to show his skill. A third man, who seemed the elder by quite twenty years, was at the window reading a newspaper; and I got no shock when I saw that it was the *Saturday Review*, which he and a laborer on an adjoining farm took in weekly between them. There was a copy of a local newspaper—the *People's Journal*—also lying about, and some books, including one of Darwin's. These were all the property of this man, however, who did the reading for the bothy.

They did all the cooking for themselves, living largely on milk. In the old days, which the senior could remember, porridge was so universally the morning meal that they called it by that name instead of breakfast. They still breakfast on porridge, but often take tea "above it." Generally milk is taken with the porridge; but "porter" or stout in a bowl is no uncommon substitute. Potatoes at twelve o'clock—seldom "brose" nowadays—are the staple dinner dish, and the tinned meats have become very popular. There are bothies where each man makes his own food; but of course the more satisfactory plan is for them to club together. Sometimes they get their food in the farm-kitchen; but this is only when there are few of them and the farmer and his family do not think it beneath them to dine with the men. Broth, too, may be made in the kitchen and sent down to the bothy. At harvest time the workers take their food in the fields, when great quantities of milk are provided. There is very little beer drunk, and whiskey is only consumed in privacy.

Life in the bothies is not, I should say, so lonely as life at the school-house, for the hands have at least each other's company. The hawker visits them frequently still, though the itinerant tailor, once a familiar figure, has almost vanished. Their great place of congregating is still some country smiddy, which is also their frequent meeting-place when bent on black-fishing. The flare of the black-fisher's torch still attracts salmon to their death in the rivers near Thrums; and you may hear in the glens on a dark night the rattle of the spears on the wet stones. Twenty or thirty years ago, however, the sport was much more common. After the farmer had gone to bed, some half-dozen ploughmen and a few other poachers from Thrums would set out for the meeting-place.

The smithy on these occasions must have been a weird sight; though one did not mark that at the time. The poacher crept from the darkness into the glaring smithy light; for in country parts the anvil might sometimes be heard clanging at all hours of the night. As a rule, every face was blackened; and it was this, I suppose, rather than the fact that dark nights were chosen, that gave the gangs the name of black-fishers. Other disguises were resorted to; one of the commonest being to change clothes or to turn your corduroys outside in. The country-folk of those days were more superstitious than they are now, and it did not take much to turn the black-fishers back. There was not a barn or byre in the district that had not its horseshoe over the door. Another popular device for frightening away witches and fairies was to hang bunches of garlic about the farms. I have known a black-fishing expedition stopped because a "yellow yite," or yellow-hammer, hovered round the gang when they were setting out. Still more ominous was the "peat" when it appeared with one or three companions. An old rhyme about this bird runs—"One is joy, two is grief, three's a bridal, four is death." Such snatches of superstition are still to be heard amidst the gossip of a north-country smithy.

Each black-fisher brought his own spear and torch, both more or less home-made. The spears were in many cases "gully-knives," fastened to staves with twine and resin, called "rozet." The torches were very rough-and-ready things—rope and tar, or even rotten roots dug from broken trees—in fact, anything that would flare. The black-fishers seldom journeyed far from home, confining themselves to the rivers within a radius of three or four miles. There were many reasons for this: one of them being that the hands had to be at their work on the farm by five o'clock in the morning: another, that so they poached and let poach. Except when in spate, the river I specially refer to offered no attractions to the black-fishers. Heavy rains, however, swell it much more quickly than most rivers into a turbulent rush of water; the part of it affected by the black-fishers being banked in with rocks that prevent the water's spreading. Above these rocks, again, are heavy green banks, from which stunted trees grow aslant across the river. The effect is fearsome at some points where the trees run into each other, as it were, from opposite banks. However, the black-fishers thought nothing of these things. They took a turnip lantern with them—that is, a lantern hollowed out of a turnip, with a piece of candle inside—but no lights were shown on the road. Every one knew his way to the river blindfold; so that the darker the night the better. On reaching the water there was a pause. One or two of the gang climbed the banks to discover if any bailiffs were on the watch; while the others sat down, and with the help of the turnip lantern "busked" their spears; in other words, fastened on the steel—or, it might be, merely pieces of rusty iron sharpened into a point at home—to the staves. Some had them busked before they set out, but that was not considered prudent; for of course there was always a risk of meeting spoil-sports on the way, to whom the spears would tell a tale that could not be learned from ordinary staves. Nevertheless little time was lost. Five or six of the gang waded into the water, torch in one hand and spear in the other; and the object now was to catch some salmon with the least possible delay, and hurry away. Windy nights were good for the sport, and I can still see the river lit up with the lumps of light that a torch makes in a high wind. The torches, of course, were used to attract the fish, which came swimming to the sheen, and were then speared. As little noise as possible was made; but though the men bit their lips instead of crying out when they missed their fish, there was a continuous ring of their weapons on the stones, and every irrepressible imprecation was echoed up and down the black glen. Two or three of the gang were told off to land the salmon, and they had to work smartly and deftly. They kept by the side of the spears-man, and the moment he struck a fish they grabbed at it with their hands. When the spear had a barb there was less chance of the fish's being lost; but often this was not the case, and probably not more than two-thirds of the salmon speared were got safely to the bank. The takes of course varied; sometimes, indeed, the black-fishers returned home empty-handed.

Encounters with the bailiffs were not infrequent, though they seldom took place at the water's edge. When the poachers were caught in the act, and had their blood up with the excitement of the sport, they were ugly customers. Spears were used and heads were broken. Struggles even took place in the water, when there was always a chance of somebody's being drowned. Where the bailiffs gave the black-fishers an opportunity of escaping without a fight it was nearly always taken; the booty being left behind. As a rule, when the "water watchers," as the bailiffs were sometimes called, had an inkling of what was to take place, they reinforced themselves with a constable or two and waited on the road to catch the poachers on their way home. One black-fisher, a noted character, was nicknamed the "Deil o' Glen Quharity." He was said to have gone to the houses of the bailiffs and offered to sell them the fish stolen from the streams over which they kept guard. The "Deil" was never imprisoned—partly, perhaps, because he was too eccentric to be taken seriously.

CHAPTER III

THE AULD LICHT KIRK

One Sabbath day in the beginning of the century the Auld Licht minister at Thrums walked out of his battered, ramshackle, earthen-floored kirk with a following and never returned. The last words he uttered in it were: "Follow me to the commonty, all you persons who want to hear the Word of God properly preached; and James Duphie and his two sons will answer for this on the Day of Judgment." The congregation, which belonged to the body who seceded from the Established Church a hundred and fifty years ago, had split, and as the New Lights (now the U.P.'s) were in the majority, the Old Lights, with the minister at their head, had to retire to the commonty (or common) and hold service in the open air until they had saved up money for a church. They kept possession, however, of the white manse among the trees. Their kirk has but a cluster of members now, most of them old and done, but each is equal to a dozen ordinary churchgoers, and there have been men and women among them on whom memory loves to linger. For forty years they have been dying out, but their cold, stiff pews still echo the Psalms of David, and the Auld Licht kirk will remain open so long as it has one member and a minister.

The church stands round the corner from the square, with only a large door to distinguish it from the other buildings in the short street. Children who want to do a brave thing hit this door with their fists, when there is no one near, and then run away scared. The door, however, is sacred to the memory of a white-haired old lady who, not so long ago, used to march out of the kirk and remain on the pavement until the psalm which had just been given out was sung. Of Thrums' pavement it may here be said that when you come, even to this day, to a level slab you will feel reluctant to leave it. The old lady was Mistress (which is Miss) Tibbie McQuhatty, and she nearly split the Auld Licht kirk over "run line." This conspicuous innovation was introduced by Mr. Dishart, the minister, when he was young and audacious. The old, reverent custom in the kirk was for the precentor to read out the psalm a line at a time. Having then sung that line he read out the next one, led the singing of it, and so worked his way on to line three. Where run line holds, however, the psalms is read out first, and forthwith sung. This is not only a flighty way of doing things, which may lead to greater scandals, but has its practical disadvantages, for the precentor always starts singing in advance of the congregation (Auld Lichts never being able to begin to do anything all at once), and, increasing the distance with every line, leaves them hopelessly behind at the finish. Miss McQuhatty protested against this change, as meeting the devil half way, but the minister carried his point, and ever after that she rushed ostentatiously from the church the moment a psalm was given out, and remained behind the door until the singing was finished, when she returned, with a rustle, to her seat. Run line had on her the effect of the reading of the Riot Act. Once some men, capable of anything, held the door from the outside, and the congregation heard Tibbie rampaging in the passage. Bursting into the kirk she called the office-bearers to her assistance, whereupon the minister in miniature raised his voice and demanded the why and wherefore of the ungodly disturbance. Great was the hubbub, but the door was fast, and a compromise had to be arrived at. The old lady consented for once to stand in the passage, but not without pressing her hands to her ears. You may smile at Tibbie, but ah! I know what she was at a sick bedside. I have seen her when the hard look had gone from her eyes, and it would ill become me to smile too.

As with all the churches in Thrums, care had been taken to make the Auld Licht one much too large. The stair to the "laft" or gallery, which was originally little more than ladder, is ready for you as soon as you enter the doorway, but it is best to sit in the body of the kirk. The plate for collections is inside the church, so that the whole congregation can give a guess at what you give. If it is something very stingy or very liberal, all Thrums knows of it within a few hours; indeed, this holds good of all the churches, especially perhaps of the Free one, which has been called the bawbee kirk, because so many halfpennies find their way into the plate. On Saturday nights the Thrums shops are besieged for coppers by housewives of all denominations, who would as soon think of dropping a threepenny bit into the plate as of giving nothing. Tammy Todd had a curious way of tipping his penny into the Auld Licht plate while still keeping his hand to his side. He did it much as a boy fires a marble, and there was quite a talk in the congregation the first time he missed. A devout plan was to carry your penny in your hand all the way to church, but to appear to take it out of your pocket on entering, and some plumped it down noisily like men paying their way. I believe old Snecky Hobart, who was a canty stock but obstinate, once dropped a penny into the plate and took out a halfpenny as change, but the only untoward thing that happened to the plate was once when the lassie from the farm of Curly Bog capsized it in passing. Mr. Dishart, who was always a ready man, introduced something into his sermon that day about women's dress, which every one hoped Christy Lundy, the lassie in question, would remember. Nevertheless, the minister sometimes came to a sudden stop himself when passing from the vestry to the pulpit. The passage being narrow, his rigging would catch in a pew as he sailed down the aisle. Even then, however, Mr. Dishart remembered that he was not as other men.

White is not a religious color, and the walls of the kirk were of a dull gray. A cushion was allowed to the manse pew, but merely as a symbol of office, and this was the only pew in the church that had a door. It was and is the pew nearest to the pulpit on the minister's right, and one day it contained a bonnet, which Mr. Dishart's predecessor preached at for one hour and ten minutes. From the pulpit, which was swaddled in black, the minister had a fine sweep of all the congregation except those in the back pews downstairs, who were lost in the shadow of the laft. Here sat Whinny Webster, so called because, having an inexplicable passion against them, he devoted his life to the extermination of whins. Whinny for years ate peppermint lozenges with impunity in his back seat, safe in the certainty that the minister, however much he might try, could not possibly see him. But his day came. One afternoon the kirk smelt of peppermints, and Mr. Dishart could rebuke no one, for the defaulter was not in sight. Whinny's cheek was working up and down in quiet enjoyment of its lozenge, when he started, noticing that the preaching had stopped. Then he heard a sepulchral voice say "Charles Webster!" Whinny's eyes turned to the pulpit, only part of which was visible to him, and to his horror they encountered the minister's head coming down the stairs. This took place after I had ceased to attend the Auld Licht kirk regularly; but I am told that as Whinny gave one wild scream the peppermint dropped from his mouth. The minister had got him by leaning over the pulpit door until, had he given himself only another inch, his feet would have gone into the air. As for Whinny he became a God-fearing man.

The most uncanny thing about the kirk was the precentor's box beneath the pulpit. Three Auld Licht ministers I have known, but I can only conceive one precentor. Lang Tammas' box was much too small for him. Since his disappearance from Thrums I believe they have paid him the compliment of enlarging it for a smaller man, no doubt with the feeling that Tammas alone could look like a Christian in it. Like the whole congregation, of course, he had to stand during the prayers—the first of which averaged half an hour in length. If he stood erect his head and shoulders vanished beneath funereal trappings, when he seemed decapitated, and if he stretched his neck the pulpit tottered. He looked like the pillar on which it rested, or he balanced it on his head like a baker's tray.

Sometimes he leaned forward as reverently as he could, and then, with his long, lean arms dangling over the side of his box, he might have been a suit of "blacks" hung up to dry. Once I was talking with Cree Queery in a sober, respectable manner, when all at once a light broke out on his face. I asked him what he was laughing at, and he said it was at Lang Tammas. He got grave again when I asked him what there was in Lang Tammas to smile at, and admitted that he could not tell me. However, I have always been of opinion that the thought of the precentor in his box gave Cree a fleeting sense of humor.

Tammas and Hendry Munn were the two paid officials of the church, Hendry being kirk-officer; but poverty was among the few points they had in common. The precentor was a cobbler, though he never knew it, shoemaker being the name in those parts, and his dwelling-room was also his workshop. There he sat in his "brot," or apron, from early morning to far on to midnight, and contrived to make his six or eight shillings a week. I have often sat with him in the darkness that his "cruizey" lamp could not pierce, while his mutterings to himself of "ay, ay, yes, umpha, oh ay, ay man," came as regularly and monotonously as the tick of his "wag-at-the-wa'" clock. Hendry and he were paid no fixed sum for their services in the Auld Licht kirk, but once a year there was a collection for each of them, and so they jogged along. Though not the only kirk-officer of my time Hendry made the most lasting impression. He was, I think, the only man in Thrums who did not quake when the minister looked at him. A wild story, never authenticated, says that Hendry once offered Mr. Dishart a snuff from his mull. In the streets Lang Tammas was more stern and dreaded by evil-doers, but Hendry had first place in the kirk. One of his duties was to precede the minister from the session-house to the pulpit and open the door for him. Having shut Mr. Dishart in he strolled away to his seat. When a strange minister preached, Hendry was, if possible, still more at his ease. This will not be believed, but I have seen him give the pulpit-door on these occasions a fling to with his feet. However ill an ordinary member of the congregation might become in the kirk he sat on till the service ended, but Hendry would wander to the door and shut it if he noticed that the wind was playing irreverent tricks with the pages of Bibles, and proof could still be brought forward that he would stop deliberately in the aisle to lift up a piece of paper, say, that had floated there. After the first psalm had been sung it was Hendry's part to lift up the plate and carry its tinkling contents to the session-house. On the greatest occasions he remained so calm, so indifferent, so expressionless, that he might have been present the night before at a rehearsal.

When there was preaching at night the church was lit by tallow candles, which also gave out all the artificial heat provided. Two candles stood on each side of the pulpit, and others were scattered over the church, some of them fixed into holes on rough brackets, and some merely sticking in their own grease on the pews. Hendry superintended the lighting of the candles, and frequently hobbled through the church to snuff them. Mr. Dishart was a man who could do anything except snuff a candle, but when he stopped in his sermon to do that he as often as not knocked the candle over. In vain he sought to refix it in its proper place, and then all eyes turned to Hendry. As coolly as though he were in a public hall or place of entertainment, the kirk-officer arose and, mounting the stair, took the candle from the minister's reluctant hands and put it right. Then he returned to his seat, not apparently puffed up, yet perhaps satisfied with himself; while Mr. Dishart, glaring after him to see if he was carrying his head high, resumed his wordy way.

Never was there a man more uncomfortably loved than Mr. Dishart. Easie Haggart, his maid-servant, reproved him at the breakfast table. Lang Tammas and Sam'l Mealmaker crouched for five successive Sabbath nights on his manse-wall to catch him smoking (and got him). Old wives grumbled by their hearths when he did not look in to despair of their salvation. He told the maidens of his congregation not to make an idol of him. His session saw him (from behind a haystack) in conversation with a strange woman, and asked grimly if he remembered that he had a wife. Twenty were his years when he came to Thrums, and on the very first Sabbath he knocked a board out of the pulpit. Before beginning his trial sermon he handed down the big Bible to the precentor, to give his arms free swing. The congregation, trembling with exhilaration, probed his meaning. Not a square inch of paper, they saw, could be concealed there. Mr. Dishart had scarcely any hope for the Auld Lichts; he had none for any other denomination. Davit Lunan got behind his handkerchief to think for a moment, and the minister was on him like a tiger. The call was unanimous. Davit proposed him.

Every few years, as one might say, the Auld Licht kirk gave way and buried its minister. The congregation turned their empty pockets inside out, and the minister departed in a farmer's cart. The scene was not an amusing one to those who looked on at it. To the Auld Lichts was then the humiliation of seeing their pulpit "supplied" on alternate Sabbaths by itinerant probationers or stickit ministers. When they were not starving themselves to support a pastor the Auld Lichts were saving up for a stipend. They retired with compressed lips to their looms, and weaved and weaved till they weaved another minister. Without the grief of parting with one minister there could not have been the transport of choosing another. To have had a pastor always might have made them vain-glorious.

They were seldom longer than twelve months in making a selection, and in their haste they would have passed over Mr. Dishart and mated with a monster. Many years have elapsed since Providence flung Mr. Watts out of the Auld Licht kirk. Mr. Watts was a probationer who was tried before Mr. Dishart, and, though not so young as might have been wished, he found favor in many eyes. "Sluggard in the laft, awake!" he cried to Bell Whamond, who had forgotten herself, and it was felt that there must be good stuff in him. A breeze from Heaven exposed him on Communion Sabbath.

On the evening of this solemn day the door of the Auld Licht kirk was sometimes locked, and the congregation repaired,

Bible in hand, to the commonty. They had a right to this common on the Communion Sabbath, but only took advantage of it when it was believed that more persons intended witnessing the evening service than the kirk would hold. On this day the attendance was always very great.

It was the Covenanters come back to life. To the summit of the slope a wooden box was slowly hurled by Hendry Munn and others, and round this the congregation quietly grouped to the tinkle of the cracked Auld Licht bell. With slow, majestic tread the session advanced upon the steep common with the little minister in their midst. He had the people in his hands now, and the more he squeezed them the better they were pleased. The travelling pulpit consisted of two compartments, the one for the minister and the other for Lang Tammas, but no Auld Licht thought that it looked like a Punch and Judy puppet show. This service on the common was known as the "tent preaching," owing to a tent's being frequently used instead of the box.

Mr. Watts was conducting the service on the commonty. It was a fine, still summer evening, and loud above the whisper of the burn from which the common climbs, and the labored "pechs" of the listeners, rose the preacher's voice. The Auld Lichts in their rusty blacks (they must have been a more artistic sight in the olden days of blue bonnets and knee-breeches) nodded their heads in sharp approval, for though they could swoop down on a heretic like an eagle on carrion, they scented no prey. Even Lang Tammas, on whose nose a drop of water gathered when he was in his greatest fettle, thought that all was fair and above-board. Suddenly a rush of wind tore up the common, and ran straight at the pulpit. It formed in a sieve, and passed over the heads of the congregation, who felt it as a fan, and looked up in awe. Lang Tammas, feeling himself all at once grow clammy, distinctly heard the leaves of the pulpit Bible shiver. Mr. Watts' hands, outstretched to prevent a catastrophe, were blown against his side, and then some twenty sheets of closely written paper floated into the air. There was a horrible, dead silence. The burn was roaring now. The minister, if such he can be called, shrank back in his box, and as if they had seen it printed in letters of fire on the heavens, the congregation realized that Mr. Watts, whom they had been on the point of calling, read his sermon. He wrote it out on pages the exact size of those in the Bible, and did not scruple to fasten these into the Holy Book itself. At theatres a sullen thunder of angry voices behind the scene represents a crowd in a rage, and such a low, long-drawn howl swept the common when Mr. Watts was found out. To follow a pastor who "read" seemed to the Auld Lichts like claiming heaven on false pretences. In ten minutes the session alone, with Lang Tammas and Hendry, were on the common. They were watched by many from afar off, and (when one comes to think of it now) looked a little curious jumping, like trout at flies, at the damning papers still fluttering in the air. The minister was never seen in our parts again, but he is still remembered as "Paper Watts."

Mr. Dishart in the pulpit was the reward of his upbringing. At ten he had entered the university. Before he was in his teens he was practising the art of gesticulation in his father's gallery pew. From distant congregations people came to marvel at him. He was never more than comparatively young. So long as the pulpit trappings of the kirk at Thrums lasted he could be seen, once he was fairly under way with his sermon, but dimly in a cloud of dust. He introduced headaches. In a grand transport of enthusiasm he once flung his arms over the pulpit and caught Lang Tammas on the forehead. Leaning forward, with his chest on the cushions, he would pommel the Evil One with both hands, and then, whirling round to the left, shake his fist at Bell Whamond's neckerchief. With a sudden jump he would fix Pete Todd's youngest boy catching flies at the laft window. Stiffening unexpectedly, he would leap three times in the air, and then gather himself in a corner for a fearsome spring. When he wept he seemed to be laughing, and he laughed in a paroxysm of tears. He tried to tear the devil out of the pulpit rails. When he was not a teetotum he was a windmill. His pump position was the most appalling. Then he glared motionless at his admiring listeners, as if he had fallen into a trance with his arm upraised. The hurricane broke next moment. Nanny Sutie bore up under the shadow of the windmill—which would have been heavier had Auld Licht ministers worn gowns—but the pump affected her to tears. She was stone-deaf.

For the first year or more of his ministry an Auld Licht minister was a mouse among cats. Both in the pulpit and out of it they watched for unsound doctrine, and when he strayed they took him by the neck. Mr. Dishart, however, had been brought up in the true way, and seldom gave his people a chance. In time, it may be said, they grew despondent, and settled in their uncomfortable pews with all suspicion of lurking heresy allayed. It was only on such Sabbaths as Mr. Dishart changed pulpits with another minister that they cocked their ears and leaned forward eagerly to snap the preacher up.

Mr. Dishart had his trials. There was the split in the kirk, too, that comes once at least to every Auld Licht minister. He was long in marrying. The congregation were thinking of approaching him, through the medium of his servant, Easie Haggart, on the subject of matrimony; for a bachelor coming on for twenty-two, with an income of eighty pounds per annum, seemed an anomaly—when one day he took the canal for Edinburgh and returned with his bride. His people nodded their heads, but said nothing to the minister. If he did not choose to take them into his confidence, it was no affair of theirs. That there was something queer about the marriage, however, seemed certain. Sandy Whamond, who was a soured man after losing his eldership, said that he believed she had been an "Englishy"—in other words, had belonged to the English Church; but it is not probable that Mr. Dishart would have gone the length of that. The secret is buried in his grave.

Easie Haggart jagged the minister sorely. She grew loquacious with years, and when he had company would stand at the door joining in the conversation. If the company was another minister, she would take a chair and discuss Mr. Dishart's infirmities with him. The Auld Lichts loved their minister, but they saw even more clearly than himself the necessity for his humiliation. His wife made all her children's clothes, but Sanders Gow complained that she looked too like their sister. In one week three of the children died, and on the Sabbath following it rained. Mr. Dishart preached, twice breaking down altogether and gaping strangely round the kirk (there was no dust flying that day), and spoke of the rain as angels' tears for three little girls. The Auld Lichts let it pass, but, as Lang Tammas said in private (for, of course, the thing was much discussed at the looms), if you materialize angels in that way, where are you going to stop?

It was on the fast-days that the Auld Licht kirk showed what it was capable of, and, so to speak, left all the other churches in Thrums far behind. The fast came round once every summer, beginning on a Thursday, when all the looms were hushed, and two services were held in the kirk of about three hours' length each. A minister from another town assisted at these times, and when the service ended the members filed in at one door and out at another, passing on their way Mr. Dishart and his elders, who dispensed "tokens" at the foot of the pulpit. Without a token, which was a metal lozenge, no one could take the sacrament on the coming Sabbath, and many a member has Mr. Dishart made miserable by refusing him his token for gathering wild-flowers, say, on a Lord's Day (as testified to by another member). Women were lost who cooked dinners on the Sabbath, or took to colored ribbons, or absented themselves from church without sufficient cause. On the fast-day fists were shaken at Mr. Dishart as he walked sternly homeward, but he was undismayed. Next day there were no services in the kirk, for Auld Lichts could not afford many holidays, but they weaved solemnly, with Saturday and the Sabbath and Monday to think of. On Saturday service began at two and lasted until nearly seven. Two sermons were preached, but there was no interval. The sacrament was dispensed on the Sabbath. Nowadays the "tables" in the Auld Licht kirk are soon "served," for the attendance has decayed, and most of the pews in the body of the church are made use of. In the days of which I speak, however, the front pews alone were hung with white, and it was in them only the sacrament was administered. As many members as could get into them delivered up their tokens and took the first table. Then they made room for others, who sat in their pews awaiting their turn. What with tables, the preaching, and unusually long prayers, the service lasted from eleven to six. At half-past six a two hours' service began, either in the kirk or on the common, from which no one who thought much about his immortal soul would have dared (or cared) to absent himself. A four hours' service on the Monday, which, like that of the Saturday, consisted of two services in one, but began at eleven instead of two, completed the programme.

On those days, if you were a poor creature and wanted to acknowledge it, you could leave the church for a few minutes and return to it, but the creditable thing was to sit on. Even among the children there was a keen competition, fostered by their parents, to sit each other out, and be in at the death.

The other Thrums kirks held the sacrament at the same time, but not with the same vehemence. As far north from the school-house as Thrums is south of it, nestles the little village of Quharity, and there the fast-day was not a day of fasting. In most cases the people had to go many miles to church. They drove or rode (two on a horse), or walked in from other glens. Without "the tents," therefore, the congregation, with a long day before them, would have been badly off. Sometimes one tent sufficed; at other times rival publicans were on the ground. The tents were those in use at the feeing and other markets, and you could get anything inside them, from broth made in a "boiler" to the firiest whiskey. They were planted just outside the kirk-gate—long, low tents of dirty white canvas—so that when passing into the church or out of it you inhaled their odors. The congregation emerged austerely from the church, shaking their heads solemnly over the minister's remarks, and their feet carried them into the tent. There was no mirth, no unseemly revelry, but there was a great deal of hard drinking. Eventually the tents were done away with, but not until the services on the fast-days were shortened. The Auld Licht ministers were the only ones who preached against the tents with any heart, and since the old dominie, my predecessor at the school-house, died, there has not been an Auld Licht permanently resident in the glen of Quharity.

Perhaps nothing took it out of the Auld Licht males so much as a christening. Then alone they showed symptoms of nervousness, more especially after the remarkable baptism of Eppie Whamond. I could tell of several scandals in connection with the kirk. There was, for instance, the time when Easie Haggart saved the minister. In a fit of temporary mental derangement the misguided man had one Sabbath day, despite the entreaties of his affrighted spouse, called at the post-office, and was on the point of reading the letter there received when Easie, who had slipped on her bonnet and followed him, snatched the secular thing from his hands. There was the story that ran like fire through Thrums and crushed an innocent man, to the effect that Pete Todd had been in an Edinburgh theatre countenancing the play-actors. Something could be made, too, of the retribution that came to Charlie Ramsay, who woke in his pew to discover that its other occupant, his little son Jamie, was standing on the seat divesting himself of his clothes in presence of a horrified congregation. Jamie had begun stealthily, and had very little on when Charlie seized him. But having my choice of scandals I prefer the christening one—the unique case of Eppie Whamond, who was born late on Saturday night and baptized in the kirk on the following forenoon.

To the casual observer the Auld Licht always looked as if he were returning from burying a near relative. Yet when I met him hobbling down the street, preternaturally grave and occupied, experience taught me that he was preparing for a christening. How the minister would have borne himself in the event of a member of his congregation's wanting the baptism to take place at home it is not easy to say; but I shudder to think of the public prayers for the parents that would certainly have followed. The child was carried to the kirk through rain, or snow, or sleet, or wind; the father took his seat alone in the front pew, under the minister's eye, and the service was prolonged far on into the afternoon. But though the references in the sermon to that unhappy object of interest in the front pew were many and pointed, his time had not really come until the minister signed to him to advance as far as the second step of the pulpit stairs. The nervous father clenched the railing in a daze, and cowered before the ministerial heckling. From warning the minister passed to exhortation, from exhortation to admonition, from admonition to searching questioning, from questioning to prayer and wailing. When the father glanced up, there was the radiant boy in the pulpit looking as if he would like to jump down his throat. If he hung his head the minister would ask, with a groan, whether he was unprepared; and the whole congregation would sigh out the response that Mr. Dishart had hit it. When he replied audibly to the minister's uncomfortable questions, a pained look at his flippancy travelled from the pulpit all round the pews; and when he only bowed his head in answer, the minister paused sternly, and the congregation wondered what the man meant. Little wonder that Davie Haggart took to drinking when his turn came for occupying that front pew.

If wee Eppie Whamond's birth had been deferred until the beginning of the week, or humility had shown more prominently among her mother's virtues, the kirk would have been saved a painful scandal, and Sandy Whamond might have retained his eldership. Yet it was a foolish but wifely pride in her husband's official position that turned Bell Dundas' head—a wild ambition to beat all baptismal record.

Among the wives she was esteemed a poor body whose infant did not see the inside of the kirk within a fortnight of its birth. Forty years ago it was an accepted superstition in Thrums that the ghosts of children who had died before they were baptized went wailing and wringing their hands round the kirk-yard at nights, and that they would continue to do this until the crack of doom. When the Auld Licht children grew up, too, they crowed over those of their fellows whose christening had been deferred until a comparatively late date, and the mothers who had needlessly missed a Sabbath for long afterward hung their heads. That was a good and creditable birth which took place early in the week, thus allowing time for suitable christening preparations; while to be born on a Friday or a Saturday was to humiliate your parents, besides being an extremely ominous beginning for yourself. Without seeking to vindicate Bell Dundas' behavior, I may note, as an act of ordinary fairness, that, being the leading elder's wife, she was sorely tempted. Eppie made her appearance at 9:45 on a Saturday night.

In the hurry and skurry that ensued, Sandy escaped sadly to the square. His infant would be baptized eight days old—one of the longest deferred christenings of the year. Sandy was shivering under the clock when I met him accidentally, and took him home. But by that time the harm had been done. Several of the congregation had been roused from their beds to hear his lamentations, of whom the men sympathized with him, while the wives triumphed austerely over Bell Dundas. As I wrung poor Sandy's hand, I hardly noticed that a bright light showed distinctly between the shutters of his kitchen-window; but the elder himself turned pale and breathed quickly. It was then fourteen minutes past twelve.

My heart sank within me on the following forenoon, when Sandy Whamond walked, with a queer twitching face, into the front pew under a glare of eyes from the body of the kirk and the laft. An amazed buzz went round the church, followed by a pursing up of lips and hurried whisperings. Evidently Sandy had been driven to it against his own judgment. The scene is still vivid before me: the minister suspecting no guile, and omitting the admonitory stage out of compliment to the elder's standing; Sandy's ghastly face; the proud godmother (aged twelve) with the squalling baby in her arms; the horror of the congregation to a man and woman. A slate fell from Sandy's house even as he held up the babe to the minister to receive a "droukin'" of water, and Eppie cried so vigorously that her shamed godmother had to rush with her to the vestry. Now things are not as they should be when an Auld Licht infant does not quietly sit out her first service.

Bell tried for a time to carry her head high; but Sandy ceased to whistle at his loom, and the scandal was a rolling stone that soon passed over him. Briefly it amounted to this: that a bairn born within two hours of midnight on Saturday could not have been ready for christening at the kirk next day without the breaking of the Sabbath. Had the secret of the nocturnal light been mine alone all might have been well; but Betsy Mund's evidence was irrefutable. Great had been Bell's cunning, but Betsy had outwitted her. Passing the house on the eventful night, Betsy had observed Marget Dundas, Bell's sister, open the door and creep cautiously to the window, the chinks in the outside shutters of which she cunningly closed up with "tow." As in a flash the disgusted Betsy saw what Bell was up to, and, removing the tow, planted herself behind the dilapidated dyke opposite and awaited events. Questioned at a special meeting of the office-bearers in the vestry, she admitted that the lamp was extinguished soon after twelve o'clock, though the fire burned brightly all night. There had been unnecessary feasting during the night, and six eggs were consumed before breakfast-time. Asked how she knew this, she admitted having counted the eggshells that Marget had thrown out of doors in the morning. This, with the testimony of the persons from whom Sandy had sought condolence on the Saturday night, was the case for the prosecution. For the defence, Bell maintained that all preparations stopped when the clock struck twelve, and even hinted that the bairn had been born on Saturday afternoon. But Sandy knew that he and his had got a fall. In the forenoon of the following Sabbath the minister preached from the text, "Be sure your sin will find you out;" and in the afternoon from "Pride goeth before a fall." He was grand. In the evening Sandy tendered his resignation of office, which was at once accepted. Webs were behind-hand for a week, owing to the length of the prayers offered up for Bell; and Lang Tammas ruled in Sandy's stead.

CHAPTER IV

LADS AND LASSES

With the severe Auld Lichts the Sabbath began at six o'clock on Saturday evening. By that time the gleaming shuttle was at rest, Davie Haggart had strolled into the village from his pile of stones in the Whunny road; Hendry Robb, the "dummy," had sold his last barrowful of "rozetty (resiny) roots" for firewood; and the people, having tranquilly supped and soused their faces in their water-pails, slowly donned their Sunday clothes. This ceremony was common to all; but here divergence set in. The gray Auld Licht, to whom love was not even a name, sat in his high-backed arm-chair by the hearth, Bible or "Pilgrim's Progress" in hand, occasionally lapsing into slumber. But—though, when they got the chance, they went willingly three times to the kirk—there were young men in the community so flighty that, instead of dozing at home on Saturday night, they dandered casually into the square, and, forming into knots at the corners, talked solemnly and mysteriously of women.

Not even, on the night preceding his wedding was an Auld Licht ever known to stay out after ten o'clock. So weekly conclaves at street-corners came to an end at a comparatively early hour, one Coelebs after another shuffling silently from the square until it echoed, deserted, to the town-house clock. The last of the gallants, gradually discovering that he was alone, would look around him musingly, and, taking in the situation, slowly wend his way home. On no other night of the week was frivolous talk about the softer sex indulged in, the Auld Lichts being creatures of habit, who never thought of smiling on a Monday. Long before they reached their teens they were earning their keep as herds in the surrounding glens or filling "pirns" for their parents; but they were generally on the brink of twenty before they thought seriously of matrimony. Up to that time they only trifled with the other sex's affections at a distance—filling a maid's water-pails, perhaps, when no one was looking, or carrying her wob; at the recollection of which they would slap their knees almost jovially on Saturday night. A wife was expected to assist at the loom as well as to be cunning in the making of marmalade and the firing of bannocks, and there was consequently some heartburning among the lads for maids of skill and muscle. The Auld Licht, however, who meant marriage seldom loitered in the streets. By-and-bye there came a time when the clock looked down through its cracked glass upon the hemmed-in square and saw him not. His companions, gazing at each other's boots, felt that something was going on, but made no remark.

A month ago, passing through the shabby, familiar square, I brushed against a withered old man tottering down the street under a load of yarn. It was piled on a wheelbarrow, which his feeble hands could not have raised but for the rope of yarn that supported it from his shoulders; and though Auld Licht was written on his patient eyes, I did not immediately recognize Jamie Whamond. Years ago Jamie was a sturdy weaver and fervent lover, whom I had the right to call my friend. Turn back the century a few decades, and we are together on a moonlight night, taking a short cut through the fields from the farm of Craigiebuckle. Buxom were Craigiebuckle's "dochters," and Jamie was Janet's accepted suitor. It was a muddy road through damp grass, and we picked our way silently over its ruts and pools. "I'm thinkin'," Jamie said at last, a little wistfully, "that I micht hae been as weel wi' Chirsty." Chirsty was Janet's sister, and Jamie had first thought of her. Craigiebuckle, however, strongly advised him to take Janet instead, and he consented. Alack! heavy wobs have taken all the grace from Janet's shoulders this many a year, though she and Jamie go bravely down the hill together. Unless they pass the allotted span of life, the "poors-house" will never know them. As for bonny Chirsty, she proved a flighty thing, and married a deacon in the Established Church. The Auld Lichts groaned over her fall, Craigiebuckle hung his head, and the minister told her sternly to go her way. But a few weeks afterward Lang Tammas, the chief elder, was observed talking with her for an hour in Gowrie's close; and the very next Sabbath Chirsty pushed her husband in triumph into her father's pew. The minister, though completely taken by surprise, at once referred to the stranger, in a prayer of great length, as a brand that might yet be plucked from the burning. Changing his text, he preached at him; Lang Tammas, the precentor, and the whole congregation (Chirsty included) sang at him; and before he exactly realized his position he had become an Auld Licht for life. Chirsty's triumph was complete when, next week, in broad daylight, too, the minister's wife called, and (in the presence of Betsy Munn, who vouches for the truth of the story) graciously asked her to come up to the manse on Thursday, at 4 P.M., and drink a dish of tea. Chirsty, who knew her position, of course begged modestly to be excused; but a coolness arose over the invitation between her and Janet—who felt slighted—that was only made up at the laying-out of Chirsty's father-in-law, to which Janet was pleasantly invited.

When they had red up the house, the Auld Licht lassies sat in the gloaming at their doors on three-legged stools, patiently knitting stockings. To them came stiff-limbed youths who, with a "Blawy nicht, Jeanie" (to which the inevitable answer was, "It is so, Cha-rles"), rested their shoulders on the doorpost, and silently followed with their eyes the flashing needles. Thus the courtship began—often to ripen promptly into marriage, at other times to go no farther. The smooth-haired maids, neat in their simple wrappers, knew they were on their trial, and that it behoved them to be wary. They had not compassed twenty winters without knowing that Marget Todd lost Davie Haggart because she "fittit" a black stocking with brown worsted, and that Finny's grieve turned from Bell Whamond on account of the frivolous flowers in her bonnet: and yet Bell's prospects, as I happen to know, at one time looked bright and promising. Sitting over her father's peat-fire one night gossiping with him about fishing-flies and tackle, I noticed the grieve, who had dropped in by appointment with some ducks' eggs on which Bell's clockin' hen was to sit, performing some sleight-of-hand trick with his coat-sleeve. Craftily he jerked and twisted it, till his own photograph (a black smudge on white) gradually appeared to view. This he gravely slipped into the hands of the maid of his choice, and then took his departure, apparently much relieved. Had not Bell's light-headedness driven him away, the grieve would have soon followed up his gift with an offer of his hand. Some night Bell would have "seen him to the door," and they would have stared sheepishly at each other before saying good-night. The parting salutation given, the grieve would still have stood his ground, and Bell would have waited with him. At last, "Will ye hae's, Bell?" would have dropped from his half-reluctant lips; and Bell would have mumbled, "Ay," with her thumb in her mouth. "Guid nicht to ye, Bell," would be the next remark—"Guid nicht to ye, Jeames," the answer; the humble door would close softly, and Bell and her lad would have been engaged. But, as it was, their attachment never got beyond the silhouette stage, from which, in the ethics of the Auld Lichts, a man can draw back in certain circumstances without loss of honor. The only really tender thing I ever heard an Auld Licht lover say to his sweetheart was when Gowrie's brother looked softly into Easie Tamson's eyes and whispered, "Do you swite (sweat)?" Even then the effect was produced more by the loving cast in Gowrie's eye than by the tenderness of the words themselves.

The courtships were sometimes of long duration, but as soon as the young man realized that he was courting he proposed. Cases were not wanting in which he realized this for himself, but as a rule he had to be told of it.

There were a few instances of weddings among the Auld Lichts that did not take place on Friday. Betsy Munn's brother thought to assert his two coal-carts, about which he was sinfully puffed up, by getting married early in the week; but he was a pragmatical feckless body, Jamie. The foreigner from York that Finny's grieve after disappointing Jinny Whamond took, sought to sow the seeds of strife by urging that Friday was an unlucky day; and I remember how the minister, who was always great in a crisis, nipped the bickering in the bud by adducing the conclusive fact that he had been married on the sixth day of the week himself. It was a judicious policy on Mr. Dishart's part to take vigorous action at once and insist on the solemnization of the marriage on a Friday or not at all, for he best kept superstition out of the congregation by branding it as heresy. Perhaps the Auld Lichts were only ignorant of the grieve's lass' theory because they had not thought of it. Friday's claims, too, were incontrovertible; for the Saturday's being a slack day gave the couple an opportunity to put their but and ben in order, and on Sabbath they had a gay day of it—three times at the kirk. The honeymoon over, the racket of the loom began again on the Monday.

The natural politeness of the Allardice family gave me my invitation to Tibbie's wedding. I was taking tea and cheese early one wintry afternoon with the smith and his wife, when little Joey Todd in his Sabbath clothes peered in at the passage, and then knocked primly at the door. Andra forgot himself, and called out to him to come in by; but Jess frowned him into silence, and, hastily donning her black mutch, received Willie on the threshold. Both halves of the door were open, and the visitor had looked us over carefully before knocking; but he had come with the compliments of Tibbie's mother, requesting the pleasure of Jess and her man that evening to the lassie's marriage with Sam'l Todd, and the knocking at the door was part of the ceremony. Five minutes afterward Joey returned to beg a moment of me in the passage; when I, too, got my invitation. The lad had just received, with an expression of polite surprise, though he knew he could claim it as his right, a slice of crumbling shortbread, and taken his staid departure, when Jess cleared the tea-things off the table, remarking simply that it was a mercy we had not got beyond the first cup. We then retired to dress.

About six o'clock, the time announced for the ceremony, I elbowed my way through the expectant throng of men, women, and children that already besieged the smith's door. Shrill demands of "Toss, toss!" rent the air every time Jess' head showed on the window-blind, and Andra hoped, as I pushed open the door, "that I hadna forgotten my bawbees." Weddings were celebrated among the Auld Lichts by showers of ha'pence, and the guests on their way to the bride's house had to scatter to the hungry rabble like housewives feeding poultry. Willie Todd, the best man, who had never come out so strong in his life before, slipped through the back window, while the crowd, led on by Kitty McQueen, seethed in front, and making a bolt for it to the "'Sosh," was back in a moment with a handful of small change. "Dinna toss ower lavishly at first," the smith whispered me nervously, as we followed Jess and Willie into the darkening wynd.

The guests were packed hot and solemn in Johnny Allardice's "room:" the men anxious to surrender their seats to the ladies who happened to be standing, but too bashful to propose it; the ham and the fish frizzling noisily side by side but the house, and hissing out every now and then to let all whom it might concern know that Janet Craik was adding more water to the gravy. A better woman never lived; but, oh, the hypocrisy of the face that beamed greeting to the guests as if it had nothing to do but politely show them in, and gasped next moment with upraised arms over what was nearly a fall in crockery. When Janet sped to the door her "spleet new" merino dress fell, to the pulling of a string, over her home-made petticoat, like the drop-scene in a theatre, and rose as promptly when she returned to slice the bacon. The murmur of admiration that filled the room when she entered with the minister was an involuntary tribute to the spotlessness of her wrapper and a great triumph for Janet. If there is an impression that the dress of the Auld Lichts was on all occasions as sombre as their faces, let it be known that the bride was but one of several in "whites," and that Mag Munn had only at the last moment been dissuaded from wearing flowers. The minister, the Auld Lichts congratulated themselves, disapproved of all such decking of the person and bowing of the head to idols; but on such an occasion he was not expected to observe it. Bell Whamond, however, has reason for knowing that, marriages or no marriages, he drew the line at curls.

By-and-bye Sam'l Todd, looking a little dazed, was pushed into the middle of the room to Tibbie's side, and the minister raised his voice in prayer. All eyes closed reverently, except perhaps the bridegroom's, which seemed glazed and vacant. It was an open question in the community whether Mr. Dishart did not miss his chance at weddings; the men shaking their heads over the comparative brevity of the ceremony, the women worshipping him (though he never hesitated to rebuke them when they showed it too openly) for the urbanity of his manners. At that time, however, only a minister of such experience as Mr. Dishart's predecessor could lead up to a marriage in prayer without inadvertently joining the couple; and the catechizing was mercifully brief. Another prayer followed the union; the minister waived his right to kiss the bride; every one looked at every other one as if he had for the moment forgotten what he was on the point of saying and found it very annoying; and Janet signed frantically to Willie Todd, who nodded intelligently in reply, but evidently had no idea what she meant. In time Johnny Allardice, our host, who became more and more and doited as the night proceeded, remembered his instructions, and led the way to the kitchen, where the guests, having politely informed their hostess that they were not hungry, partook of a hearty tea. Mr. Dishart presided, with the bride and bridegroom near him; but though he tried to give an agreeable turn to the conversation by describing the extensions at the cemetery, his personality oppressed us, and we only breathed freely when he rose to go. Yet we marvelled at his versatility. In shaking hands with the newly married couple the minister reminded them that it was leap-year, and wished them "three hundred and sixty-six happy and God-fearing days."

Sam'l's station being too high for it, Tibbie did not have a penny wedding, which her thrifty mother bewailed, penny weddings starting a couple in life. I can recall nothing more characteristic of the nation from which the Auld Lichts sprang than the penny wedding, where the only revellers that were not out of pocket by it were the couple who gave the entertainment. The more the guests ate and drank the better, pecuniarily, for their hosts. The charge for admission to the penny wedding (practically to the feast that followed it) varied in different districts, but with us it was generally a shilling. Perhaps the penny extra to the fiddler accounts for the name penny wedding. The ceremony having been gone through in the bride's house, there was an adjournment to a barn or other convenient place of meeting, where was held the nuptial feast; long white boards from Rob Angus' saw-mill, supported on trestles, stood in lieu of tables; and those of the company who could not find a seat waited patiently against the wall for a vacancy. The shilling gave every guest the free run of the groaning board; but though fowls were plentiful, and even white bread too, little had been spent on them. The farmers of the neighborhood, who looked forward to providing the young people with drills of potatoes for the coming winter, made a bid for their custom by sending them a fowl gratis for the marriage supper. It was popularly understood to be the oldest cock of the farmyard, but for all that it made a brave appearance in a shallow sea of soup. The fowls were always boiled—without exception, so far as my memory carries me; the guid-wife never having the heart to roast them, and so lose the broth. One round of whiskey-and-water was all the drink to which his shilling entitled the guest. If he wanted more he had to pay for it. There was much revelry, with song and dance, that no stranger could have thought those stiff-limbed weavers capable of; and the more they shouted and whirled through the barn, the more their host smiled and rubbed his hands. He presided at the bar improvised for the occasion, and if the thing was conducted with spirit his bride flung an apron over her gown and helped him. I remember one elderly bridegroom who, having married a blind woman, had to do double work at his penny wedding. It was a sight to see him flitting about the torch-lit barn, with a kettle of hot water in one hand and a besom to sweep up crumbs in the other.

Though Sam'l had no penny wedding, however, we made a night of it at his marriage.

Wedding-chariots were not in those days, though I know of Auld Lichts being conveyed to marriages nowadays by horses with white ears. The tea over, we formed in couples, and—the best man with the bride, the bridegroom with the best maid, leading the way—marched in slow procession in the moonlight night to Tibbie's new home, between lines of hoarse and eager onlookers. An attempt was made by an itinerant musician to head the company with his fiddle; but instrumental music, even in the streets, was abhorrent to sound Auld Lichts, and the minister had spoken privately to Willie Todd on the subject. As a consequence, Peter was driven from the ranks. The last thing I saw that night, as we filed, bareheaded and solemn, into the newly married couple's house, was Kitty McQueen's vigorous arm, in a dishevelled sleeve, pounding a pair of urchins who had got between her and a muddy ha'penny.

That night there was revelry and boisterous mirth (or what the Auld Lichts took for such) in Tibbie's kitchen. At eleven o'clock Davit Lunan cracked a joke. Davie Haggart, in reply to Bell Dundas' request, gave a song of distinctly secular tendencies. The bride (who had carefully taken off her wedding-gown on getting home and donned a wrapper) coquettishly let the bridegroom's father hold her hand. In Auld Licht circles, when one of the company was offered whiskey and refused it, the others, as if pained even at the offer, pushed it from them as a thing abhorred. But Davie Haggart set another example on this occasion, and no one had the courage to refuse to follow it. We sat late round the dying fire, and it was only Willie Todd's scandalous assertion (he was but a boy) about his being able to dance that induced us to think of moving. In the community, I understand, this marriage is still memorable as the occasion on which Bell Whamond laughed in the minister's face.

CHAPTER V

THE AULD LIGHTS IN ARMS

Arms and men I sing: douce Jeemsy Todd, rushing from his loom, armed with a bed-post; Lisbeth Whamond, an avenging whirlwind: Neil Haggart, pausing in his thank-offerings to smite and slay; the impious foe scudding up the bleeding Brae-head with Nemesis at their flashing heels; the minister holding it a nice question whether the carnage was not justified. Then came the two hours' sermons of the following Sabbath, when Mr. Dishart, revolving like a teetotum in the pulpit, damned every bandaged person present, individually and collectively; and Lang Tammas in the precentor's box with a plaster on his cheek, included any one the minister might have by chance omitted, and the congregation, with most of their eyes bunged up, burst into psalms of praise.

Twice a year the Auld Lichts went demented. The occasion was the fast-day at Tilliedrum; when its inhabitants, instead of crowding reverently to the kirk, swooped profanely down in their scores and tens of scores on our God-fearing town, intent on making a day of it. Then did the weavers rise as one man, and go forth to show the ribald crew the errors of their way. All denominations were represented, but Auld Lichts led. An Auld Licht would have taken no man's blood without the conviction that he would be the better morally for the bleeding; and if Tammas Lunan's case gave an impetus to the blows, it can only have been because it opened wider Auld Licht eyes to Tilliedrum's desperate condition. Mr. Dishart's predecessor more than once remarked that at the Creation the devil put forward a claim for Thrums, but said he would take his chance of Tilliedrum; and the statement was generally understood to be made on the authority of the original Hebrew.

The mustard-seed of a feud between the two parishes shot into a tall tree in a single night, when Davit Lunan's father went to a tattie roup at Tilliedrum and thoughtlessly died there. Twenty-four hours afterward a small party of staid Auld Lichts, carrying long white poles, stepped out of various wynds and closes and picked their solemn way to the house of mourning. Nanny Low, the widow, received them dejectedly, as one oppressed by the knowledge that her man's death at such an inopportune place did not fulfil the promise of his youth; and her guests admitted bluntly that they were disappointed in Tammas. Snecky Hobart's father's unusually long and impressive prayer was an official intimation that the deceased, in the opinion of the session, sorely needed everything of the kind he could get; and then the silent driblet of Auld Lichts in black stalked off in the direction of Tilliedrum. Women left their spinning-wheels and pirns to follow them with their eyes along the Tenements, and the minister was known to be holding an extra service at the manse. When the little procession reached the boundary-line between the two parishes, they sat down on a dyke and waited.

By-and-bye half a dozen men drew near from the opposite direction, bearing on poles the remains of Tammas Lunan in a closed coffin. The coffin was brought to within thirty yards of those who awaited it, and then roughly lowered to the ground. Its bearers rested morosely on their poles. In conveying Lunan's remains to the borders of his own parish they were only conforming to custom; but Thrums and Tilliedrum differed as to where the boundary-line was drawn, and not a foot would either advance into the other's territory.

For half a day the coffin lay unclaimed, and the two parties sat scowling at each other. Neither dared move. Gloaming had stolen into the valley when Dite Deuchars, of Tilliedrum, rose to his feet and deliberately spat upon the coffin. A stone whizzed through the air; and then the ugly spectacle was presented, in the gray night, of a dozen mutes fighting with their poles over a coffin. There was blood on the shoulders that bore Tammas' remains to Thrums.

After that meeting Tilliedrum lived for the fast-day. Never, perhaps, was there a community more given up to sin, and Thrums felt "called" to its chastisement. The insult to Lunan's coffin, however, dispirited their weavers for a time, and not until the suicide of Pitlums did they put much fervor into their prayers. It made new men of them. Tilliedrum's sins had found it out. Pitlums was a farmer in the parish of Thrums, but he had been born at Tilliedrum; and Thrums thanked Providence for that, when it saw him suspended between two hams from his kitchen rafters. The custom was to cart suicides to the quarry at the Galla pond and bury them near the cairn that had supported the gallows; but on this occasion not a farmer in the parish would lend a cart, and for a week the corpse lay on the sanded floor as it had been cut down—an object of awestruck interest to boys who knew no better than to peep through the darkened window. Tilliedrum bit its lips at home. The Auld Licht minister, it was said, had been approached on the subject; but, after serious consideration, did not see his way to offering up a prayer. Finally old Hobart and two others tied a rope round the body, and dragged it from the farm to the cairn, a distance of four miles. Instead of this incident's humbling Tilliedrum into attending church, the next fast-day saw its streets deserted. As for the Thrums Auld Lichts, only heavy wobs prevented their walking erect like men who had done their duty. If no prayer was volunteered for Pitlums before his burial, there was a great deal of psalm-singing after it.

By early morn on their fast-day the Tilliedrummers were straggling into Thrums, and the weavers, already at their looms, read the clattering of feet and carts aright. To convince themselves, all they had to do was to raise their eyes; but the first triumph would have been to Tilliedrum if they had done that. The invaders—the men in Aberdeen blue serge coats, velvet knee-breeches, and broad blue bonnets, and the wincey gowns of the women set off with hooded cloaks of red or tartan—tapped at the windows and shouted insultingly as they passed; but, with pursed lips, Thrums bent fiercely over its wobs, and not an Auld Licht showed outside his door. The day wore on to noon, and still ribaldry was master of the wynds. But there was a change inside the houses. The minister had pulled down his blinds; moody men had left their looms for stools by the fire; there were rumors of a conflict in Andra Gowrie's close, from which Kitty McQueen had emerged with her short gown in rags; and Lang Tammas was going from door to door. The austere precentor admonished fiery youth to beware of giving way to passion; and it was a proud day for the Auld Lichts to find their leading elder so conversant with apt Scripture texts. They bowed their heads reverently while he thundered forth that those who lived by the sword would perish by the sword; and when he had finished they took him ben to inspect their bludgeons. I have a vivid recollection of going the round of the Auld Licht and other houses to see the sticks and the wrists in coils of wire.

A stranger in the Tenements in the afternoon would have noted more than one draggled youth in holiday attire, sitting on a doorstep with a wet cloth to his nose; and, passing down the commonty, he would have had to step over prostrate lumps of humanity from which all shape had departed. Gavin Ogilvy limped heavily after his encounter with Thrummy Tosh—a struggle that was looked forward to eagerly as a bi-yearly event; Christy Davie's development of muscle had not prevented her going down before the terrible onslaught of Joe the miller, and Lang Tammas' plasters told a tale. It was in the square that the two parties, leading their maimed and blind, formed in force; Tilliedrum thirsting for its opponents' blood, and Thrums humbly accepting the responsibility of punching the fast-day breakers into the ways of rectitude. In the small, ill-kept square the invaders, to the number of about a hundred, were wedged together at its upper end, while the Thrums people formed in a thick line at the foot. For its inhabitants the way to Tilliedrum lay through this threatening mass of armed weavers. No words were bandied between the two forces; the centre of the square was left open, and nearly every eye was fixed on the town-house clock. It directed operations and gave the signal to charge. The moment six o'clock struck, the upper mass broke its bonds and flung itself on the living barricade. There was a clatter of heads and sticks, a yelling and a groaning, and then the invaders, bursting through the opposing ranks, fled for Tilliedrum. Down the Tanage brae and up the Brae-head they skurried, half a hundred avenging spirits in pursuit. On the Tilliedrum fast-day I have tasted blood myself. In the godless place there is no Auld Licht kirk, but there are two Auld Lichts in it now who walk to Thrums to church every Sabbath, blow or rain as it lists. They are making their influence felt in Tilliedrum.

The Auld Lichts also did valorous deeds at the Battle of Cabbylatch. The farm land so named lies a mile or more to the south of Thrums. You have to go over the rim of the cut to reach it. It is low-lying and uninteresting to the eye, except for some giant stones scattered cold and naked through the fields. No human hands reared these bowlders, but they might be looked upon as tombstones to the heroes who fell (to rise hurriedly) on the plain of Cabbylatch.

The fight of Cabbylatch belongs to the days of what are now but dimly remembered as the Meal Mobs. Then there was a wild cry all over the country for bread (not the fine loaves that we know, but something very much coarser), and hungry men and women, prematurely shrunken, began to forget the taste of meal. Potatoes were their chief sustenance, and, when the crop failed, starvation gripped them. At that time the farmers, having control of the meal, had the small towns at their mercy, and they increased its cost. The price of the meal went up and up, until the famishing people swarmed up the sides of the carts in which it was conveyed to the towns, and, tearing open the sacks, devoured it in handfuls. In Thrums they had a stern sense of justice, and for a time, after taking possession of the meal, they carried it to the square and sold it at what they considered a reasonable price. The money was handed over to the farmers. The honesty of this is worth thinking about, but it seems to have only incensed the farmers the more; and when they saw that to send their meal to the town was not to get high prices for it, they laid their heads together and then gave notice that the people who wanted meal and were able to pay for it must come to the farms. In Thrums no one who cared to live on porridge and bannocks had money to satisfy the farmers; but, on the other hand, none of them grudged going for it, and go they did. They went in numbers from farm to farm, like bands of hungry rats, and throttled the opposition they not infrequently encountered. The raging farmers at last met in council, and, noting that they were lusty men and brave, resolved to march in armed force upon the erring people and burn their town. Now we come to the Battle of Cabbylatch.

The farmers were not less than eighty strong, and chiefly consisted of cavalry. Armed with pitchforks and cumbrous scythes where they were not able to lay their hands on the more orthodox weapons of war, they presented a determined appearance; the few foot-soldiers who had no cart-horses at their disposal bearing in their arms bundles of firewood. One memorable morning they set out to avenge their losses; and by and by a halt was called, when each man bowed his head to listen. In Thrums, pipe and drum were calling the inhabitants to arms. Scouts rushed in with the news that the farmers were advancing rapidly upon the town, and soon the streets were clattering with feet. At that time Thrums had its piper and drummer (the bellman of a later and more degenerate age); and on this occasion they marched together through the narrow wynds, firing the blood of haggard men and summoning them to the square. According to my informant's father, the gathering of these angry and startled weavers, when he thrust his blue bonnet on his head and rushed out to join them, was an impressive and solemn spectacle. That bloodshed was meant there can be no doubt; for starving men do not see the ludicrous side of things. The difference between the farmers and the town had resolved itself into an ugly and sullen hate, and the wealthier townsmen who would have come between the people and the bread were fiercely pushed aside. There was no nominal leader, but every man in the ranks meant to fight for himself and his belongings; and they are said to have sallied out to meet the foe in no disorder. The women they would fain have left behind them; but these had their own injuries to redress, and they followed in their husbands' wake carrying bags of stones. The men, who were of various denominations, were armed with sticks, blunderbusses, anything they could snatch up at a moment's notice; and some of them were not unacquainted with fighting. Dire silence prevailed among the men, but the women shouted as they ran, and the curious army moved forward to the drone and squall of drum and pipe. The enemy was sighted on the level land of Cabbylatch, and here, while the intending combatants glared at each other, a well-known local magnate galloped his horse between them and ordered them in the name of the king to return to their homes. But for the farmers that meant further depredation at the people's hands, and the townsmen would not go back to their gloomy homes to sit down and wait for sunshine. Soon stones (the first, it is said, cast by a woman) darkened the air. The farmers got the word to charge, but their horses, with the best intentions, did not know the way. There was a stampeding in different directions, a blind rushing of one frightened steed against another; and then the townspeople, breaking any ranks they had hitherto managed to keep, rushed vindictively forward. The struggle at Cabbylatch itself was not of long duration; for their own horses proved the farmers' worst enemies, except in the cases where these sagacious animals took matters into their own ordering and bolted judiciously for their stables. The day was to Thrums.

Individual deeds of prowess were done that day. Of these not the least fondly remembered by her descendants were those of the gallant matron who pursued the most obnoxious farmer in the district even to his very porch with heavy stones and opprobrious epithets. Once when he thought he had left her far behind did he alight to draw breath and take a pinch of snuff, and she was upon him like a flail. With a terror stricken cry he leaped once more upon his horse and fled, but not without leaving his snuff-box in the hands of the derisive enemy. Meggy has long gone to the kirk-yard, but the snuff-mull is still preserved.

Some ugly cuts were given and received, and heads as well as ribs were broken; but the townsmen's triumph was short-lived. The ringleaders were whipped through the streets of Perth, as a warning to persons thinking of taking the law into their own hands; and all the lasting consolation they got was that, some time afterward, the chief witness against them, the parish minister, met with a mysterious death. They said it was evidently the hand of God; but some people looked suspiciously at them when they said it.

CHAPTER VI

THE OLD DOMINIE

From the new cemetery, which is the highest point in Thrums, you just fail to catch sight of the red school-house that nestles between two bare trees, some five miles up the glen of Quharity. This was proved by Davit Lunan, tinsmith, whom I have heard tell the story. It was in the time when the cemetery gates were locked to keep the bodies of suicides out, but men who cared to risk the consequences could get the coffin over the high dyke and bury it themselves. Peter Lundy's coffin broke, as one might say, into the church-yard in this way, Peter having hanged himself in the Whunny wood when he saw that work he must. The general feeling among the intimates of the deceased was expressed by Davit when he said:

"It may do the crittur nae guid i' the tail o' the day, but he paid for's bit o' ground, an' he's in's richt to occupy it."

The custom was to push the coffin on to the wall up a plank, and then let it drop less carefully into the cemetery. Some of the mourners were dragging the plank over the wall, with Davit Lunan on the top directing them, when they seem to have let go and sent the tinsmith suddenly into the air. A week afterward it struck Davit, when in the act of soldering a hole in Leeby Wheens' flagon (here he branched off to explain that he had made the flagon years before, and that Leeby was sister to Tammas Wheens, and married one Baker Robbie, who died of chicken-pox in his forty-fourth year), that when "up there" he had a view of Quharity school-house. Davit was as truthful as a man who tells the same story more than once can be expected to be, and it is far from a suspicious circumstance that he did not remember seeing the school-house all at once. In Thrums things only struck them gradually. The new cemetery, for instance, was only so called because it had been new once.

In this red stone school, full of the modern improvements that he detested, the old dominie whom I succeeded taught, and sometimes slept, during the last five years of his cantankerous life. It was in a little thatched school, consisting of but one room, that he did his best work, some five hundred yards away from the edifice that was reared in its stead. Now dismally fallen into disrepute, often indeed a domicile for cattle, the ragged academy of Glen Quharity, where he held despotic sway for nearly half a century, is falling to pieces slowly in a howe that conceals it from the high-road. Even in its best scholastic days, when it sent barefooted lads to college who helped to hasten the Disruption, it was but a pile of ungainly stones, such as Scott's Black Dwarf flung together in a night, with holes in its broken roof of thatch where the rain trickled through, and never with less than two of its knotted little window-panes stopped with brown paper. The twelve or twenty pupils of both sexes who constituted the attendance sat at the two loose desks, which never fell unless you leaned on them, with an eye on the corner of the earthen floor where the worms came out, and on cold days they liked the wind to turn the peat smoke into the room. One boy, who was supposed to wash it out, got his education free for keeping the school-house dirty, and the others paid their way with peats, which they brought in their hands, just as wealthier school-children carry books, and with pence which the dominie collected regularly every Monday morning. The attendance on Monday mornings was often small.

Once a year the dominie added to his income by holding cockfights in the old school. This was at Yule, and the same practice held in the parish school of Thrums. It must have been a strange sight. Every male scholar was expected to bring a cock to the school, and to pay a shilling to the dominie for the privilege of seeing it killed there. The dominie was the master of the sports, assisted by the neighboring farmers, some of whom might be elders of the church. Three rounds were fought. By the end of the first round all the cocks had fought, and the victors were then pitted against each other. The cocks that survived the second round were eligible for the third, and the dominie, besides his shilling, got every cock killed. Sometimes, if all stories be true, the spectators were fighting with each other before the third round concluded.

The glen was but sparsely dotted with houses even in those days; a number of them inhabited by farmer-weavers, who combined two trades and just managed to live. One would have a plough, another a horse, and so in Glen Quharity they helped each other. Without a loom in addition many of them would have starved, and on Saturdays the big farmer and his wife, driving home in a gig, would pass the little farmer carrying or wheeling his wob to Thrums. When there was no longer a market for the produce of the hand-loom these farms had to be given up, and thus it is that the old school is not the only house in our weary glen around which gooseberry and currant bushes, once tended by careful hands, now grow wild.

In heavy spates the children were conveyed to the old school, as they are still to the new one, in carts, and between it and the dominie's whitewashed, dwelling-house swirled in winter a torrent of water that often carried lumps of the land along with it. This burn he had at times to ford on stilts.

Before the Education Act passed the dominie was not much troubled by the school inspector, who appeared in great splendor every year at Thrums. Fifteen years ago, however, Glen Quharity resolved itself into a School Board, and marched down the glen, with the minister at its head, to condemn the school. When the dominie, who had heard of their design, saw the board approaching, he sent one of his scholars, who enjoyed making a mess of himself, wading across the burn to bring over the stilts which were lying on the other side. The board were thus unable to send across a spokesman, and after they had harangued the dominie, who was in the best of tempers, from the wrong side of the stream, the siege was raised by their returning home, this time with the minister in the rear. So far as is known, this was the only occasion on which the dominie ever lifted his hat to the minister. He was the Established Church minister at the top of the glen, but the dominie was an Auld Licht, and trudged into Thrums to church nearly every Sunday with his daughter.

The farm of Little Tilly lay so close to the dominie's house that from one window he could see through a telescope whether the farmer was going to church, owing to Little Tilly's habit of never shaving except with that intention, and of always doing it at a looking-glass which he hung on a nail in his door. The farmer was Established Church, and when the dominie saw him in his shirt-sleeves with a razor in his hand, he called for his black clothes. If he did not see him it is undeniable that the dominie sent his daughter to Thrums, but remained at home himself. Possibly, therefore, the dominie sometimes went to church, because he did not want to give Little Tilly and the Established minister the satisfaction of knowing that he was not devout today, and it is even conceivable that had Little Tilly had a telescope and an intellect as well as his neighbor, he would have spied on the dominie in return. He sent the teacher a load of potatoes every year, and the recipient rated him soundly if they did not turn out as well as the ones he had got the autumn before. Little Tilly was rather in awe of the dominie, and had an idea that he was a Freethinker, because he played the fiddle and wore a black cap.

The dominie was a wizened-looking little man, with sharp eyes that pierced you when they thought they were unobserved, and if any visitor drew near who might be a member of the board, he disappeared into his house much as a startled weasel makes for its hole. The most striking thing about him was his walk, which to the casual observer seemed a limp. The glen in our part is marshy, and to progress along it you have to jump from one little island of grass or heather to another. Perhaps it was this that made the dominie take the main road and even the streets of Thrums in leaps, as if there were bowlders or puddles in the way. It is, however, currently believed among those who knew him best that he jerked himself along in that way when he applied for the vacancy in Glen Quharity school, and that he was therefore chosen from among the candidates by the committee of farmers, who saw that he was specially constructed for the district.

In the spring the inspector was sent to report on the school, and, of course, he said, with a wave of his hand, that this would never do. So a new school was built, and the ramshackle little academy that had done good service in its day was closed for the last time. For years it had been without a lock; ever since a blatter of wind and rain drove the door against the fire-place. After that it was the dominie's custom, on seeing the room cleared, to send in a smart boy—a dux was always chosen—who wedged a clod of earth or peat between doorpost and door. Thus the school was locked up for the night. The boy came out by the window, where he entered to open the door next morning. In time grass hid the little path from view that led to the old school, and a dozen years ago every particle of wood about the building, including the door and the framework of the windows, had been burned by travelling tinkers.

The board would have liked to leave the dominie in his whitewashed dwelling-house to enjoy his old age comfortably, and until he learned that he had intended to retire. Then he changed his tactics and removed his beard. Instead of railing at the new school, he began to approve of it, and it soon came to the ears of the horrified Established minister, who had a man (Established) in his eye for the appointment, that the dominie was looking ten years younger. As he spurned a pension he had to get the place, and then began a warfare of bickerings between the board and him that lasted until within a few weeks of his death. In his scholastic barn the dominie had thumped the Latin grammar into his scholars till they became university bursars to escape him. In the new school, with maps (which he hid in the hen-house) and every other modern appliance for making teaching easy, he was the scandal of the glen. He snapped at the clerk of the board's throat, and barred his door in the minister's face. It was one of his favorite relaxations to peregrinate the district, telling the farmers who were not on the board themselves, but were given to gossiping with those who were, that though he could slumber pleasantly in the school so long as the hum of the standards was kept up, he immediately woke if it ceased.

Having settled himself in his new quarters, the dominie seems to have read over the code and come at once to the conclusion that it would be idle to think of straightforwardly fulfilling its requirements. The inspector he regarded as a natural enemy, who was to be circumvented by much guile. One year that admirable Oxford don arrived at the school, to find that all the children, except two girls—one of whom had her face tied up with red flannel—were away for the harvest. On another occasion the dominie met the inspector's trap some distance from the school, and explained that he would guide him by a short cut, leaving the driver to take the dog-cart to a farm where it could be put up. The unsuspecting inspector agreed, and they set off, the obsequious dominie carrying his bag. He led his victim into another glen, the hills round which had hidden their heads in mist, and then slyly remarked that he was afraid they had lost their way. The minister, who liked to attend the examination, reproved the dominie for providing no luncheon, but turned pale when his enemy suggested that he should examine the boys in Latin.

For some reason that I could never discover, the dominie had all his life refused to teach his scholars geography. The inspector and many others asked him why there was no geography class, and his invariable answer was to point to his pupils collectively, and reply in an impressive whisper:

"They winna hae her."

This story, too, seems to reflect against the dominie's views on cleanliness. One examination day the minister attended to open the inspection with prayer. Just as he was finishing, a scholar entered who had a reputation for dirt.

"Michty!" cried a little pupil, as his opening eyes fell on the apparition at the door, "there's Jocky Tamson wi' his face washed!"

When the dominie was a younger man he had first clashed with the minister during Mr. Rattray's attempts to do away with some old customs that were already dying by inches. One was the selection of a queen of beauty from among the young women at the annual Thrums fair. The judges, who were selected from the better-known farmers as a rule, sat at the door of a tent that reeked of whiskey, and regarded the competitors filing by much as they selected prize sheep, with a stolid stare. There was much giggling and blushing on these occasions among the maidens, and shouts from their relatives and friends to "Haud yer head up, Jean," and "Lat them see yer een, Jess." The dominie enjoyed this, and was one time chosen, a judge, when he insisted on the prize's being bestowed on his own daughter, Marget. The other judges demurred, but the dominie remained firm and won the day.

"She wasna the best-faured amon them," he admitted afterward, "but a man maun mak the maist o' his ain."

The dominie, too, would not shake his head with Mr. Rattray over the apple and loaf bread raffles in the smithy, nor even at the Daft Days, the black week of glum debauch that ushered in the year, a period when the whole countryside rumbled to the farmers' "kebec" laden cart.

For the great part of his career the dominie had not made forty pounds a year, but he "died worth" about three hundred pounds. The moral of his life came in just as he was leaving it, for he rose from his death-bed to hide a whiskey-bottle from his wife.

CHAPTER VII

CREE QUEERY AND MYSY DROLLY

The children used to fling stones at Grinder Queery because he loved his mother. I never heard the Grinder's real name. He and his mother were Queery and Drolly, contemptuously so called, and they answered to these names. I remember Cree best as a battered old weaver, who bent forward as he walked, with his arms hanging limp as if ready to grasp the shafts of the barrow behind which it was his life to totter up hill and down hill, a rope of yarn suspended round his shaking neck and fastened to the shafts, assisting him to bear the yoke and slowly strangling him. By and by there came a time when the barrow and the weaver seemed both palsy-stricken, and Cree, gasping for breath, would stop in the middle of a brae, unable to push his load over a stone. Then he laid himself down behind it to prevent the barrow's slipping back. On those occasions only the barefooted boys who jeered at the panting weaver could put new strength into his shrivelled arms. They did it by telling him that he and Mysy would have to go to the "poorshouse" after all, at which the gray old man would wince, as if "joukin" from a blow, and, shuddering, rise and, with a desperate effort, gain the top of the incline. Small blame perhaps attached to Cree if, as he neared his grave, he grew a little dottle. His loads of yarn frequently took him past the workhouse, and his eyelids quivered as he drew near. Boys used to gather round the gate in anticipation of his coming, and make a feint of driving him inside. Cree, when he observed them, sat down on his barrow-shafts terrified to approach, and

I see them now pointing to the workhouse till he left his barrow on the road and hobbled away, his legs cracking as he ran.

It is strange to know that there was once a time when Cree was young and straight, a callant who wore a flower in his button-hole and tried to be a hero for a maiden's sake.

Before Cree settled down as a weaver, he was knife and scissor grinder for three counties, and Mysy, his mother, accompanied him wherever he went. Mysy trudged alongside him till her eyes grew dim and her limbs failed her, and then Cree was told that she must be sent to the pauper's home. After that a pitiable and beautiful sight was to be seen. Grinder Queery, already a feeble man, would wheel his grindstone along the long high-road, leaving Mysy behind. He took the stone on a few hundred yards, and then, hiding it by the roadside in a ditch or behind a paling, returned for his mother. Her he led—sometimes he almost carried her—to the place where the grindstone lay, and thus by double journeys kept her with him. Every one said that Mysy's death would be a merciful release—every one but Cree.

Cree had been a grinder from his youth, having learned the trade from his father, but he gave it up when Mysy became almost blind. For a time he had to leave her in Thrums with Dan'l Wilkie's wife, and find employment himself in Tilliedrum. Mysy got me to write several letters for her to Cree, and she cried while telling me what to say. I never heard either of them use a term of endearment to the other, but all Mysy could tell me to put in writing was: "Oh, my son Cree; oh, my beloved son; oh, I have no one but you; oh, thou God watch over my Cree!" On one of these occasions Mysy put into my hands a paper, which she said would perhaps help me to write the letter. It had been drawn up by Cree many years before, when he and his mother had been compelled to part for a time, and I saw from it that he had been trying to teach Mysy to write. The paper consisted of phrases such as "Dear son Cree," "Loving mother," "I am takin' my food weel,"

"Yesterday," "Blankets," "The peats is near done," "Mr. Dishart," "Come home, Cree." The grinder had left this paper with his mother, and she had written letters to him from it.

When Dan'l Wilkie objected to keeping a cranky old body like Mysy in his house, Cree came back to Thrums and took a single room with a hand-loom in it. The flooring was only lumpy earth, with sacks spread over it to protect Mysy's feet. The room contained two dilapidated old coffin-beds, a dresser, a high-backed arm-chair, several three-legged stools, and two tables, of which one could be packed away beneath the other. In one corner stood the wheel at which Cree had to fill his own pirns. There was a plate-rack on one wall, and near the chimney-piece hung the wag-at-the-wall clock, the time-piece that was commonest in Thrums at that time, and that got this name because its exposed pendulum swung along the wall. The two windows in the room faced each other on opposite walls, and were so small that even a child might have stuck in trying to crawl through them. They opened on hinges, like a door. In the wall of the dark passage leading from the outer door into the room was a recess where a pan and pitcher of water always stood wedded, as it were, and a little hole, known as the "bole," in the wall opposite the fire-place contained Cree's library. It consisted of Baxter's "Saints' Rest," Harvey's "Meditations," the "Pilgrim's Progress," a work on folk-lore, and several Bibles. The saut-backet, or salt-bucket, stood at the end of the fender, which was half of an old cart-wheel. Here Cree worked, whistling "Ower the watter for Chairlie" to make Mysy think that he was as gay as a mavis. Mysy grew querulous in her old age, and up to the end she thought of poor, done Cree as a handsome gallant. Only by weaving far on into the night could Cree earn as much as six shillings a week. He began at six o'clock in the morning, and worked until midnight by the light of his cruizey. The cruizey was all the lamp Thrums had in those days, though it is only to be seen in use now in a few old-world houses in the glens. It is an ungainly thing in iron, the size of a man's palm, and shaped not unlike the palm when contracted and deepened to hold a liquid. Whale-oil, lying open in the mould, was used, and the wick was a rash with the green skin peeled off. These rashes were sold by herd-boys at a halfpenny the bundle, but Cree gathered his own wicks. The rashes skin readily when you know how to do it. The iron mould was placed inside another of the same shape, but slightly larger, for in time the oil dripped through the iron, and the whole was then hung by a cleek or hook close to the person using it. Even with three wicks it gave but a stime of light, and never allowed the weaver to see more than the half of his loom at a time. Sometimes Cree used threads for wicks. He was too dull a man to have many visitors, but Mr. Dishart called occasionally and reproved him for telling his mother lies. The lies Cree told Mysy were that he was sharing the meals he won for her, and that he wore the overcoat which he had exchanged years before for a blanket to keep her warm.

There was a terrible want of spirit about Grinder Queery. Boys used to climb on to his stone roof with clods of damp earth in their hands, which they dropped down the chimney. Mysy was bedridden by this time, and the smoke threatened to choke her; so Cree, instead of chasing his persecutors, bargained with them. He gave them fly-hooks which he had busked himself, and when he had nothing left to give he tried to flatter them into dealing gently with Mysy by talking to them as men. One night it went through the town that Mysy now lay in bed all day listening for her summons to depart. According to her ideas this would come in the form of a tapping at the window, and their intention was to forestall the spirit. Dite Gow's boy, who is now a grown man, was hoisted up to one of the little windows, and he has always thought of Mysy since as he saw her then for the last time. She lay sleeping, so far as he could see, and Cree sat by the fireside looking at her.

Every one knew that there was seldom a fire in that house unless Mysy was cold. Cree seemed to think that the fire was getting low. In the little closet, which, with the kitchen, made up his house, was a corner shut off from the rest of the room by a few boards, and behind this he kept his peats. There was a similar receptacle for potatoes in the kitchen. Cree wanted to get another peat for the fire without disturbing Mysy. First he took off his boots, and made for the peats on tip-toe. His shadow was cast on the bed, however, so he next got down on his knees and crawled softly into the closet. With the peat in his hands he returned in the same way, glancing every moment at the bed where Mysy lay. Though Tammy Gow's face was pressed against a broken window, he did not hear Cree putting that peat on the fire. Some say that Mysy heard, but pretended not to do so for her son's sake; that she realized the deception he played on her and had not the heart to undeceive him. But it would be too sad to believe that. The boys left Cree alone that night.

The old weaver lived on alone in that solitary house after Mysy left him, and by and by the story went abroad that he was saving money. At first no one believed this except the man who told it, but there seemed after all to be something in it. You had only to hit Cree's trouser pocket to hear the money chinking, for he was afraid to let it out of his clutch. Those who sat on dykes with him when his day's labor was over said that the wearer kept his hand all the time in his pocket, and that they saw his lips move as he counted his hoard by letting it slip through his fingers. So there were boys who called "Miser Queery" after him instead of Grinder, and asked him whether he was saving up to keep himself from the workhouse.

But we had all done Cree wrong. It came out on his death-bed what he had been storing up his money for. Grinder, according to the doctor, died of getting a good meal from a friend of his earlier days after being accustomed to starve on potatoes and a very little oatmeal indeed. The day before he died this friend sent him half a sovereign, and when Grinder saw it he sat up excitedly in his bed and pulled his corduroys from beneath his pillow. The woman who, out of kindness, attended him in his last illness, looked on curiously while Cree added the sixpences and coppers in his pocket to the half-sovereign. After all they only made some two pounds, but a look of peace came into Cree's eyes as he told the woman to take it all to a shop in the town. Nearly twelve years previously

Jamie Lownie had lent him two pounds, and though the money was never asked for, it preyed on Cree's mind that he was in debt. He paid off all he owed, and so Cree's life was not, I think, a failure.

CHAPTER VIII

THE COURTING OF T'NOWHEAD'S BELL

For two years it had been notorious in the square that Sam'l Dickie was thinking of courting T'nowhead's Bell, and that if little Sanders Elshioner (which is the Thrums pronunciation of Alexander Alexander) went in for her, he might prove a formidable rival. Sam'l was a weaver in the Tenements, and Sanders a coal-carter, whose trade-mark was a bell on his horse's neck that told when coal was coming. Being something of a public man, Sanders had not, perhaps, so high a social position as Sam'l, but he had succeeded his father on the coal-cart, while the weaver had already tried several trades. It had always been against Sam'l, too, that once when the kirk was vacant he had advised the selection of the third minister who preached for it on the ground that it came expensive to pay a large number of candidates. The scandal of the thing was hushed up, out of respect for his father, who was a God-fearing man, but Sam'l was known by it in Lang Tammas' circle. The coal-carter was called Little Sanders to distinguish him from his father, who was not much more than half his size. He had grown up with the name, and its inapplicability now came home to nobody. Sam'l's mother had been more far-seeing than Sanders'. Her man had been called Sammy all his life because it was the name he got as a boy, so when their eldest son was born she spoke of him as Sam'l while still in the cradle. The neighbors imitated her, and thus the young man had a better start in life than had been granted to Sammy, his father.

It was Saturday evening—the night in the week when Auld Licht young men fell in love. Sam'l Dickie, wearing a blue glengarry bonnet with a red ball on the top, came to the door of a one-story house in the Tenements, and stood there wriggling, for he was in a suit of tweed for the first time that week, and did not feel at one with them. When his feeling of being a stranger to himself wore off, he looked up and down the road, which straggles between houses and gardens, and then, picking his way over the puddles, crossed to his father's hen-house and sat down on it. He was now on his way to the square.

Eppie Fargus was sitting on an adjoining dyke knitting stockings, and Sam'l looked at her for a time.

"Is't yersel, Eppie?" he said at last.

"It's a' that," said Eppie.

"Hoo's a' wi' ye?" asked Sam'l.

"We're juist aff an' on," replied Eppie, cautiously.

There was not much more to say, but as Sam'l sidled off the hen-house, he murmured politely, "Ay, ay." In another minute he would have been fairly started, but Eppie resumed the conversation.

"Sam'l," she said, with a twinkle in her eye, "ye can tell Lisbeth Fargus I'll likely be drappin' in on her' aboot Mununday or Teisday."

Lisbeth was sister to Eppie, and wife of Tammas McQuhatty, better known as T'nowhead, which was the name of his farm. She was thus Bell's mistress.

Sam'l leaned against the hen-house as if all his desire to depart had gone.

"Hoo d'ye kin I'll be at the T'nowhead the nicht?" he asked, grinning in anticipation.

"Ou, I'se warrant ye'll be after Bell," said Eppie.

"Am no sae sure o' that," said Sam'l, trying to leer. He was enjoying himself now.

"Am no sure o' that," he repeated, for Eppie seemed lost in stitches.

"Sam'l!"

"Ay."

"Ye'll be speirin' her sune noo, I dinna doot?"

This took Sam'l, who had only been courting Bell for a year or two, a little aback.

"Hoo d'ye mean, Eppie?" he asked.

"Maybe ye'll do't the nicht."

"Na, there's nae hurry," said Sam'l.

"Weel, we're a' coontin' on't, Sam'l."

"Gae wa wi' ye."

"What for no?"

"Gae wa wi' ye," said Sam'l again,

"Bell's gei an' fond o' ye, Sam'l."

"Ay," said Sam'l.

"But am dootin' ye're a fell billy wi' the lasses."

"Ay, oh, I d'na kin, moderate, moderate," said Sam'l, in high delight.

"I saw ye," said Eppie, speaking with a wire in her mouth, "gae'in on terr'ble wi' Mysy Haggart at the pump last Saturday."

"We was juist amoosin' oorsels," said Sam'l,

"It'll be nae amoosement to Mysy," said Eppie, "gin ye brak her heart."

"Losh, Eppie," said Sam'l, "I didna think o' that."

"Ye maun kin weel, Sam'l, 'at there's mony a lass wid jump at ye."

"Ou, weel," said Sam'l, implying that a man must take these things as they come.

"For ye're a dainty chield to look at, Sam'l."

"Do ye think so, Eppie? Ay, ay; oh, I d'na kin am onything by the ordinar."

"Ye mayna be," said Eppie, "but lasses doesna do to be ower partikler."

Sam'l resented this, and prepared to depart again.

"Ye'll no tell Bell that?" he asked, anxiously.

"Tell her what?"

"Aboot me an' Mysy."

"We'll see hoo ye behave yersel, Sam'l."

"No 'at I care, Eppie; ye can tell her gin ye like. I widna think twice o' tellin' her mysel."

"The Lord forgie ye for leein', Sam'l," said Eppie, as he disappeared down Tammy Tosh's close. Here he came upon Henders Webster.

"Ye're late, Sam'l," said Henders.

"What for?"

"Ou, I was thinkin' ye wid be gaen the length o' T'nowhead the nicht, an' I saw Sanders Elshioner makkin's wy there an oor syne."

"Did ye?" cried Sam'l, adding craftily, "but it's naething to me."

"Tod, lad," said Henders, "gin ye dinna buckle to, Sanders'll be carryin' her off."

Sam'l flung back his head and passed on.

"Sam'l!" cried Henders after him.

"Ay," said Sam'l, wheeling round.

"Gie Bell a kiss frae me."

The full force of this joke struck neither all at once. Sam'l began to smile at it as he turned down the school-wynd, and it came upon Henders while he was in his garden feeding his ferret. Then he slapped his legs gleefully, and explained the conceit to Will'um Byars, who went into the house and thought it over.

There were twelve or twenty little groups of men in the square, which was lit by a flare of oil suspended over a cadger's cart. Now and again a staid young woman passed through the square with a basket on her arm, and if she had lingered long enough to give them time, some of the idlers would have addressed her. As it was, they gazed after her, and then grinned to each other.

"Ay, Sam'l," said two or three young men, as Sam'l joined them beneath the town-clock. "Ay, Davit," replied Sam'l.

This group was composed of some of the sharpest wits in Thrums, and it was not to be expected that they would let this opportunity pass. Perhaps when Sam'l joined them he knew what was in store for him.

"Was ye lookin' for T'nowhead's Bell, Sam'l?" asked one.

"Or mebbe ye was wantin' the minister?" suggested another, the same who had walked out twice with Chirsty Duff and not married her after all.

Sam'l could not think of a good reply at the moment, so he laughed good-naturedly.

"Ondootedly she's a snod bit crittur," said Davit, archly.

"An' michty clever wi' her fingers," added Jamie Deuchars.

"Man, I've thocht o' makkin' up to Bell mysel," said Pete Ogle. "Wid there be ony chance, think ye, Sam'l?"

"I'm thinkin' she widna hae ye for her first, Pete," replied Sam'l, in one of those happy flashes that come to some men, "but there's nae sayin' but what she micht tak ye to finish up wi'."

The unexpectedness of this sally startled every one. Though Sam'l did not set up for a wit, however, like Davit, it was notorious that he could say a cutting thing once in a way.

"Did ye ever see Bell reddin' up?" asked Pete, recovering from his overthrow. He was a man who bore no malice.

"It's a sicht," said Sam'l, solemnly.

"Hoo will that be?" asked Jamie Deuchars.

"It's weel worth yer while," said Pete, "to ging atower to the T'nowhead an' see. Ye'll mind the closed-in beds i' the kitchen? Ay, weel, they're a fell spoilt crew, T'nowhead's litlins, an' no that aisy to manage. Th' ither lasses Lisbeth's hae'n had a michty trouble wi' them. When they war i' the middle o' their reddin' up the bairns wid come tumlin' about the floor, but, sal, I assure ye, Bell didna fash lang wi' them. Did she, Sam'l?"

"She did not," said Sam'l, dropping into a fine mode of speech to add emphasis to his remark.

"I'll tell ye what she did," said Pete to the others. "She juist lifted up the litlins, twa at a time, an' flung them into the coffin-beds. Syne she snibbit the doors on them, an' keepit them there till the floor was dry."

"Ay, man, did she so?" said Davit, admiringly.

"I've seen her do't mysel," said Sam'l.

"There's no a lassie maks better bannocks this side o' Fetter Lums," continued Pete.

"Her mither tocht her that," said Sam'l; "she was a gran' han' at the bakin', Kitty Ogilvy."

"I've heard say," remarked Jamie, putting it this way so as not to tie himself down to anything, "'at Bell's scones is equal to Mag Lunan's."

"So they are," said Sam'l, almost fiercely.

"I kin she's a neat han' at singein' a hen," said Pete.

"An' wi't a'," said Davit, "she's a snod, canty bit stocky in her Sabbath claes."

"If onything, thick in the waist," suggested Jamie.

"I dinna see that," said Sam'l.

"I d'na care for her hair either," continued Jamie, who was very nice in his tastes; "something mair yalloweby wid be an improvement."

"A'body kins," growled Sam'l, "'at black hair's the bonniest." The others chuckled. "Puir Sam'l!" Pete said.

Sam'l not being certain whether this should be received with a smile or a frown, opened his mouth wide as a kind of compromise. This was position one with him for thinking things, over.

Few Auld Lichts, as I have said, went the length of choosing a helpmate for themselves. One day a young man's friends would see him mending the washing-tub of a maiden's mother. They kept the joke until Saturday night, and then he learned from them what he had been after. It dazed him for a time, but in a year or so he grew accustomed to the idea, and they were then married. With a little help he fell in love just like other people.

Sam'l was going the way of the others, but he found it difficult to come to the point. He only went courting once a week, and he could never take up the running at the place where he left off the Saturday before. Thus he had not, so far, made great headway. His method of making up to Bell had been to drop in at T'nowhead on Saturday nights and talk with the farmer about the rinderpest.

The farm kitchen was Bell's testimonial. Its chairs, tables, and stools were scoured by her to the whiteness of Rob Angus' saw-mill boards, and the muslin blind on the window was starched like a child's pinafore. Bell was brave, too, as well as energetic. Once Thrums had been overrun with thieves. It is now thought that there may have been only one, but he had the wicked cleverness of a gang. Such was his repute that there were weavers who spoke of locking their doors when they went from home. He was not very skilful, however, being generally caught, and when they said they knew he was a robber, he gave them their things back and went away. If they had given him time there is no doubt that he would have gone off with his plunder. One night he went to T'nowhead, and Bell, who slept In the kitchen, was awakened by the noise. She knew who it would be, so she rose and dressed herself, and went to look for him with a candle. The thief had not known what to do when he got in, and as it was very lonely he was glad to see Bell. She told him he ought to be ashamed of himself, and would not let him out by the door until he had taken off his boots so as not to soil the carpet.

On this Saturday evening Sam'l stood his ground in the square, until by and by he found himself alone. There were other groups there still, but his circle had melted away. They went separately, and no one said good-night. Each took himself off slowly, backing out of the group until he was fairly started.

Sam'l looked about him, and then, seeing that the others had gone, walked round the town-house into the darkness of the brae that leads down and then up to the farm of T'nowhead.

To get into the good graces of Lisbeth Fargus you had to know her ways and humor them. Sam'l, who was a student of women, knew this, and so, instead of pushing the door open and walking in, he went through the rather ridiculous ceremony of knocking. Sanders Elshioner was also aware of this weakness of Lisbeth's, but though he often made up his mind to knock, the absurdity of the thing prevented his doing so when he reached the door. T'nowhead himself had never got used to his wife's refined notions, and when any one knocked he always started to his feet, thinking there must be something wrong.

Lisbeth came to the door, her expansive figure blocking the way in.

"Sam'l," she said.

"Lisbeth," said Sam'l.

He shook hands with the farmer's wife, knowing that she liked it, but only said, "Ay, Bell," to his sweetheart, "Ay, T'nowhead," to McQuhatty, and "It's yersel, Sanders," to his rival.

They were all sitting round the fire; T'nowhead, with his feet on the ribs, wondering why he felt so warm, and Bell darned a stocking, while Lisbeth kept an eye on a goblet full of potatoes.

"Sit into the fire, Sam'l," said the farmer, not, however, making way for him.

"Na, na," said Sam'l; "I'm to bide nae time." Then he sat into the fire. His face was turned away from Bell, and when she spoke he answered her without looking round. Sam'l felt a little anxious. Sanders Elshioner, who had one leg shorter than the other, but looked well when sitting, seemed suspiciously at home. He asked Bell questions out of his own head, which was beyond Sam'l, and once he said something to her in such a low voice that the others could not catch it. T'nowhead asked curiously what it was, and Sanders explained that he had only said, "Ay, Bell, the morn's the Sabbath." There was nothing startling in this, but Sam'l did not like it. He began to wonder if he were too late, and had he seen his opportunity would have told Bell of a nasty rumor that Sanders intended to go over to the Free Church if they would make him kirk-officer.

Sam'l had the good-will of T'nowhead's wife, who liked a polite man. Sanders did his best, but from want of practice he constantly made mistakes. To-night, for instance, he wore his hat in the house because he did not like to put up his hand and take it off. T'nowhead had not taken his off either, but that was because he meant to go out by and by and lock the byre door. It was impossible to say which of her lovers Bell preferred. The proper course with an Auld Licht lassie was to prefer the man who proposed to her.

"Ye'll bide a wee, an' hae something to eat?" Lisbeth asked Sam'l, with her eyes on the goblet.

"No, I thank ye," said Sam'l, with true gentility.

"Ye'll better."

"I dinna think it."

"Hoots aye; what's to hender ye?"

"Weel, since ye're sae pressin', I'll bide."

No one asked Sanders to stay. Bell could not, for she was but the servant, and T'nowhead knew that the kick his wife had given him meant that he was not to do so either. Sanders whistled to show that he was not uncomfortable.

"Ay, then, I'll be stappin' ower the brae," he said at last.

He did not go, however. There was sufficient pride in him to get him off his chair, but only slowly, for he had to get accustomed to the notion of going. At intervals of two or three minutes he remarked that he must now be going. In the same circumstances Sam'l would have acted similarly. For a Thrums man, it is one of the hardest things in life to get away from anywhere.

At last Lisbeth saw that something must be done. The potatoes were burning, and T'nowhead had an invitation on his tongue.

"Yes, I'll hae to be movin'," said Sanders, hopelessly, for the fifth time.

"Guid nicht to ye, then, Sanders," said Lisbeth. "Gie the door a fling-to, ahent ye."

Sanders, with a mighty effort, pulled himself together. He looked boldly at Bell, and then took off his hat carefully. Sam'l saw with misgivings that there was something in it which was not a handkerchief. It was a paper bag glittering with gold braid, and contained such an assortment of sweets as lads bought for their lasses on the Muckle Friday.

"Hae, Bell," said Sanders, handing the bag to Bell in an off-hand way as if it were but a trifle. Nevertheless he was a little excited, for he went off without saying good-night.

No one spoke. Bell's face was crimson. T'nowhead fidgeted on his chair, and Lisbeth looked at Sam'l. The weaver was strangely calm and collected, though he would have liked to know whether this was a proposal.

"Sit in by to the table, Sam'l," said Lisbeth, trying to look as if things were as they had been before.

She put a saucerful of butter, salt, and pepper near the fire to melt, for melted butter is the shoeing-horn that helps over a meal of potatoes. Sam'l, however, saw what the hour required, and jumping up, he seized his bonnet.

"Hing the tatties higher up the joist, Lisbeth," he said with dignity; "I'se be back in ten meenits."

He hurried out of the house, leaving the others looking at each other.

"What do ye think?" asked Lisbeth.

"I d'na kin," faltered Bell.

"Thae tatties is lang o' comin' to the boil," said T'nowhead.

In some circles a lover who behaved like Sam'l would have been suspected of intent upon his rival's life, but neither Bell nor Lisbeth did the weaver that injustice. In a case of this kind it does not much matter what T'nowhead thought.

The ten minutes had barely passed when Sam'l was back in the farm kitchen. He was too flurried to knock this time, and, indeed, Lisbeth did not expect it of him.

"Bell, hae!" he cried, handing his sweetheart a tinsel bag twice the size of Sanders' gift.

"Losh preserve's!" exclaimed Lisbeth; "I'se warrant there's a shillin's worth."

"There's a' that, Lisbeth—an' mair," said Sam'l firmly.

"I thank ye, Sam'l," said Bell, feeling an unwonted elation as she gazed at the two paper bags in her lap.

"Ye're ower extravegint, Sam'l," Lisbeth said.

"Not at all," said Sam'l; "not at all. But I widna advise ye to eat thae ither anes, Bell—they're second quality."

Bell drew back a step from Sam'l.

"How do ye kin?" asked the farmer shortly, for he liked Sanders.

"I speired i' the shop," said Sam'l.

The goblet was placed on a broken plate on the table with the saucer beside it, and Sam'l, like the others, helped himself. What he did was to take potatoes from the pot with his fingers, peel off their coats, and then dip them into the butter. Lisbeth would have liked to provide knives and forks, but she knew that beyond a certain point T'nowhead was master in his own house. As for Sam'l, he felt victory in his hands, and began to think that he had gone too far.

In the mean time Sanders, little witting that Sam'l had trumped his trick, was sauntering along the kirk-wynd with his hat on the side of his head. Fortunately he did not meet the minister.

The courting of T'nowhead's Bell reached its crisis one Sabbath about a month after the events above recorded. The minister was in great force that day, but it is no part of mine to tell how he bore himself. I was there, and am not likely to forget the scene. It was a fateful Sabbath for T'nowhead's Bell and her swains, and destined to be remembered for the painful scandal which they perpetrated in their passion.

Bell was not in the kirk. There being an infant of six months in the house it was a question of either Lisbeth or the lassie's staying at home with him, and though Lisbeth was unselfish in a general way, she could not resist the delight of going to church. She had nine children besides the baby, and being but a woman, it was the pride of her life to march them into the T'nowhead pew, so well watched that they dared not misbehave, and so tightly packed that they could not fall. The congregation looked at that pew, the mothers enviously, when they sang the lines—

> "Jerusalem like a city is
> Compactly built together."

The first half of the service had been gone through on this particular Sunday without anything remarkable happening. It was at the end of the psalm which preceded the sermon that Sanders Elshioner, who sat near the door, lowered his head until it was no higher than the pews, and in that attitude, looking almost like a four-footed animal, slipped out of the church. In their eagerness to be at the sermon many of the congregation did not notice him, and those who did put the matter by in their minds for future investigation. Sam'l, however, could not take it so coolly. From his seat in the gallery he saw Sanders disappear, and his mind misgave him. With the true lover's instinct he understood it all. Sanders had been struck by the fine turn-out in the T'nowhead pew. Bell was alone at the farm. What an opportunity to work one's way up to a proposal! T'nowhead was so over-run with children, that such a chance seldom occurred, except on a Sabbath. Sanders, doubtless, was off to propose, and he, Sam'l, was left behind.

The suspense was terrible. Sam'l and Sanders had both known all along that Bell would take the first of the two who asked her. Even those who thought her proud admitted that she was modest. Bitterly the weaver repented having waited so long. Now it was too late. In ten minutes Sanders would be at T'nowhead; in an hour all would be over. Sam'l rose to his feet in a daze. His mother pulled him down by the coat-tail, and his father shook him, thinking he was walking in his sleep. He tottered past them, however, hurried up the aisle, which was so narrow that Dan'l Ross could only reach his seat by walking sideways, and was gone before the minister could do more than stop in the middle of a whirl and gape in horror after him.

A number of the congregation felt that day the advantage of sitting in the laft. What was a mystery to those downstairs was revealed to them. From the gallery windows they had a fine open view to the south; and as Sam'l took the common; which was a short cut though a steep ascent, to T'nowhead, he was never out of their line of vision. Sanders was not to be seen, but they guessed rightly the reason why. Thinking he had ample time, he had gone round by the main road to save his boots—perhaps a little scared by what was coming. Sam'l's design was to forestall him by taking the shorter path over the burn and up the commonty.

It was a race for a wife, and several onlookers in the gallery braved the minister's displeasure to see who won. Those who favored Sam'l's suit exultingly saw him leap the stream, while the friends of Sanders fixed their eyes on the top of the common where it ran into the road. Sanders must come into sight there, and the one who reached this point first would get Bell.

As Auld Lichts do not walk abroad on the Sabbath, Sanders would probably not be delayed. The chances were in his favor. Had it been any other day in the week Sam'l might have run. So some of the congregation in the gallery were thinking, when suddenly they saw him bend low and then take to his heels. He had caught sight of Sanders' head bobbing over the hedge that separated the road from the common, and feared that Sanders might see him. The congregation who could crane their necks sufficiently saw a black object, which they guessed to be the carter's hat, crawling along the hedge-top. For a moment it was motionless, and then it shot ahead. The rivals had seen each other. It was now a hot race. Sam'l, dissembling no longer, clattered up the common, becoming smaller and smaller to the on-lookers as he neared the top. More than one person in the gallery almost rose to their feet in their excitement. Sam'l had it. No, Sanders was in front. Then the two figures disappeared from view. They seemed to run into each other at the top of the brae, and no one could say who was first. The congregation looked at one another. Some of them perspired. But the minister held on his course.

Sam'l had just been in time to cut Sanders out. It was the weaver's saving that Sanders saw this when his rival turned the corner; for Sam'l was sadly blown. Sanders took in the situation and gave in at once. The last hundred yards of the distance he covered at his leisure, and when he arrived at his destination he did not go in. It was a fine afternoon for the time of year, and he went round to have a look at the pig, about which T'nowhead was a little sinfully puffed up.

"Ay," said Sanders, digging his fingers critically into the grunting animal; "quite so."

"Grumph," said the pig, getting reluctantly to his feet.

"Ou, ay; yes," said Sanders, thoughtfully.

Then he sat down on the edge of the sty, and looked long and silently at an empty bucket. But whether his thoughts were of T'nowhead's Bell, whom he had lost forever, or of the food the farmer fed his pig on, is not known.

"Lord preserve's! Are ye no at the kirk?" cried Bell, nearly dropping the baby as Sam'l broke into the room,

"Bell!" cried Sam'l.

Then T'nowhead's Bell knew that her hour had come.

"Sam'l," she faltered.

"Will ye hae's, Bell?" demanded Sam'l, glaring at her sheepishly.

"Ay," answered Bell.

Sam'l fell into a chair.

"Bring's a drink o' water, Bell," he said. But Bell thought the occasion required milk, and there was none in the kitchen. She went out to the byre, still with the baby in her arms, and saw Sanders Elshioner sitting gloomily on the pig-sty.

"Weel, Bell," said Sanders.

"I thocht ye'd been at the kirk, Sanders," said Bell.

Then there was a silence between them.

"Has Sam'l speired ye, Bell?" asked Sanders stolidly.

"Ay," said Bell again, and this time there was a tear in her eye.

Sanders was little better than an "orra man," and Sam'l was a weaver, and yet—But it was too late now. Sanders gave the pig a vicious poke with a stick, and when it had ceased to grunt, Bell was back in the kitchen. She had forgotten about the milk, however, and Sam'l only got water after all.

In after days, when the story of Bell's wooing was told, there were some who held that the circumstances would have almost justified the lassie in giving Sam'l the go-by. But these perhaps forgot that her other lover was in the same predicament as the accepted one—that of the two, indeed, he was the more to blame, for he set off to T'nowhead on the Sabbath of his own accord, while Sam'l only ran after him. And then there is no one to say for certain whether Bell heard of her suitors' delinquencies until Lisbeth's return from the kirk. Sam'l could never remember whether he told her, and Bell was not sure whether, if he did, she took it in. Sanders was greatly in demand for weeks after to tell what he knew of the affair, but though he was twice asked to tea to the manse among the trees, and subjected thereafter to ministerial cross-examinations, this is all he told. He remained at the pig-sty until Sam'l left the farm, when he joined him at the top of the brae, and they went home together.

"It's yersel, Sanders," said Sam'l.

"It is so, Sam'l," said Sanders.

"Very cauld," said Sam'l.

"Blawy," assented Sanders.

After a pause—

"Sam'l," said Sanders.

"Ay."

"I'm hearin' ye're to be mairit."

"Ay."

"Weel, Sam'l, she's a snod bit lassie."

"Thank ye," said Sam'l.

"I had ance a kin' o' notion o' Bell mysel," continued Sanders.

"Ye had?"

"Yes, Sam'l; but I thocht better o't."

"Hoo d'ye mean?" asked Sam'l, a little anxiously.

"Weel, Sam'l, mairitch is a terrible responsibeelity."

"It is so," said Sam'l, wincing.

"An' no the thing to tak up withoot conseederation."

"But it's a blessed and honorable state, Sanders; ye've heard the minister on't."

"They say," continued the relentless Sanders, "'at the minister doesna get on sair wi' the wife himsel."

"So they do," cried Sam'l, with a sinking at the heart.

"I've been telt," Sanders went on, "'at gin ye can get the upper han' o' the wife for a while at first, there's the mair chance o' a harmonious exeestence."

"Bell's no the lassie," said Sam'l appealingly, "to thwart her man."

Sanders smiled.

"D'ye think she is, Sanders?"

"Weel, Sam'l, I d'na want to fluster ye, but she's been ower lang wi' Lisbeth Fargus no to hae learnt her ways. An a'body kins what a life T'nowhead has wi' her."

"Guid sake, Sanders, hoo did ye no speak o' this afore?"

"I thocht ye kent o't, Sam'l."

They had now reached the square, and the U.P. kirk was coming out. The Auld Licht kirk would be half an hour yet.

"But, Sanders," said Sam'l, brightening up, "ye was on yer wy to spier her yer-sel."

"I was, Sam'l," said Sanders, "and I canna but be thankfu' ye was ower quick for's."

"Gin't hadna been you," said Sam'l, "I wid never hae thocht o't."

"I'm sayin' naething agin Bell," pursued the other, "but, man Sam'l, a body should be mair deleeberate in a thing o' the kind."

"It was michty hurried," said Sam'l, wo-fully.

"It's a serious thing to spier a lassie," said Sanders.

"It's an awfu' thing," said Sam'l.

"But we'll hope for the best," added Sanders in a hopeless voice.

They were close to the Tenements now, and Sam'l looked as if he were on his way to be hanged.

"Sam'l!"

"Ay, Sanders."

"Did ye—did ye kiss her, Sam'l?"

"Na."

"Hoo?"

"There's was varra little time, Sanders."

"Half an 'oor," said Sanders.

"Was there? Man Sanders, to tell ye the truth, I never thocht o't."

Then the soul of Sanders Elshioner was filled with contempt for Sam'l Dickie.

The scandal blew over. At first it was expected that the minister would interfere to prevent the union, but beyond intimating from the pulpit that the souls of Sabbath-breakers were beyond praying for, and then praying for Sam'l and Sanders at great length, with a word thrown in for Bell, he let things take their course. Some said it was because he was always frightened lest his young men should intermarry with other denominations, but Sanders explained it differently to Sam'l.

"I hav'na a word to say agin the minister," he said; "they're gran' prayers, but, Sam'l, he's a mairit man himsel."

"He's a' the better for that, Sanders, isna he?"

"Do ye no see," asked Sanders compassionately, "'at he's tryin' to mat the best o't?"

"Oh, Sanders, man!" said Sam'l.

"Cheer up, Sam'l," said Sanders, "it'll sune be ower."

Their having been rival suitors had not interfered with their friendship. On the contrary, while they had hitherto been mere acquaintances, they became inseparables as the wedding-day drew near. It was noticed that they had much to say to each other, and that when they could not get a room to themselves they wandered about together in the churchyard. When Sam'l had anything to tell Bell he sent Sanders to tell it, and Sanders did as he was bid. There was nothing that he would not have done for Sam'l.

The more obliging Sanders was, however, the sadder Sam'l grew. He never laughed now on Saturdays, and sometimes his loom was silent half the day. Sam'l felt that Sanders' was the kindness of a friend for a dying man.

It was to be a penny wedding, and Lisbeth Fargus said it was delicacy that made Sam'l superintend the fitting-up of the barn by deputy. Once he came to see it in person, but he looked so ill that Sanders had to see him home. This was on the Thursday afternoon, and the wedding was fixed for Friday.

"Sanders, Sanders," said Sam'l, in a voice strangely unlike his own, "it'll a' be ower by this time the morn."

"It will," said Sanders.

"If I had only kent her langer," continued Sam'l.

"It wid hae been safer," said Sanders.

"Did ye see the yallow floor in Bell's bonnet?" asked the accepted swain.

"Ay," said Sanders reluctantly.

"I'm dootin'—I'm sair dootin' she's but a flichty, light-hearted crittur after a'."

"I had ay my suspeecions o't," said Sanders.

"Ye hae kent her langer than me," said Sam'l.

"Yes," said Sanders, "but there's nae gettin' at the heart o' women. Man, Sam'l, they're desperate cunnin'."

"I'm dootin't; I'm sair dootin't."

"It'll be a warnin' to ye, Sam'l, no to be in sic a hurry i' the futur," said Sanders.

Sam'l groaned.

"Ye'll be gaein up to the manse to arrange wi' the minister the morn's mornin'," continued Sanders, in a subdued voice.

Sam'l looked wistfully at his friend.

"I canna do't, Sanders," he said, "I canna do't."

"Ye maun," said Sanders.

"It's aisy to speak," retorted Sam'l bitterly.

"We have a' oor troubles, Sam'l," said Sanders soothingly, "an' every man maun bear his ain burdens. Johnny Davie's wife's dead, an' he's no repinin'."

"Ay," said Sam'l, "but a death's no a mairitch. We hae haen deaths in our family too."

"It may a' be for the best," added Sanders, "an' there wid be a michty talk i' the hale country-side gin ye didna ging to the minister like a man."

"I maum hae langer to think o't," said Sam'l.

"Bell's mairitch is the morn," said Sanders decisively.

Sam'l glanced up with a wild look in his eyes.

"Sanders!" he cried.

"Sam'l!"

"Ye hae been a guid friend to me, Sanders, in this sair affliction."

"Nothing ava," said Sanders; "dount mention'd."

"But, Sanders, ye canna deny but what your rinnin oot o' the kirk that awfu' day was at the bottom o'd a'."

"It was so," said Sanders bravely.

"An' ye used to be fond o' Bell, Sanders."

"I dinna deny't."

"Sanders, laddie," said Sam'l, bending forward and speaking in a wheedling voice, "I aye thocht it was you she likit."

"I had some sic idea mysel," said Sanders.

"Sanders, I canna think to pairt twa fowk sae weel suited to ane anither as you an' Bell,"

"Canna ye, Sam'l?"

"She wid mak ye a guid wife, Sanders, I hae studied her weel, and she's a thrifty, douce, clever lassie. Sanders, there's no the like o' her. Mony a time, Sanders, I hae said to mysel, 'There's a lass ony man micht be prood to tak.' A'body says the same, Sanders, There's nae risk ava, man: nane to speak o'. Tak her, laddie, tak her, Sanders; it's a grand chance, Sanders. She's yours for the spierin'. I'll gie her up, Sanders."

"Will ye, though?" said Sanders.

"What d'ye think?" asked Sam'l.

"If ye wid rayther," said Sanders politely.

"There's my han' on't," said Sam'l. "Bless ye, Sanders; ye've been a true frien' to me."

Then they shook hands for the first time in their lives; and soon afterward Sanders struck up the brae to T'nowhead,

Next morning Sanders Elshioner, who had been very busy the night before, put on his Sabbath clothes and strolled up to the manse.

"But—but where is Sam'l?" asked the minister; "I must see himself."

"It's a new arrangement," said Sanders.

"What do you mean, Sanders?"

"Bell's to marry me," explained Sanders.

"But—but what does Sam'l say?"

"He's willin'," said Sanders.

"And Bell?"

"She's willin', too. She prefers't."

"It is unusual," said the minister.

"It's a' richt," said Sanders.

"Well, you know best," said the minister.

"You see the hoose was taen, at ony rate," continued Sanders. "An' I'll juist ging in til't instead o' Sam'l."

"Quite so."

"An' I cudna think to disappoint the lassie."

"Your sentiments do you credit, Sanders," said the minister; "but I hope you do not enter upon the blessed state of matrimony without full consideration of its responsibilities. It is a serious business, marriage."

"It's a' that," said Sanders, "but I'm willin' to stan' the risk."

So, as soon as it could be done, Sanders Elshioner took to wife T'nowhead's Bell, and I remember seeing Sam'l Dickie trying to dance at the penny wedding.

Years afterward it was said in Thrums that Sam'l had treated Bell badly, but he was never sure about it himself.

"It was a near thing—a michty near thing," he admitted in the square.

"They say," some other weaver would remark, "'at it was you Bell liked best."

"I d'na kin," Sam'l would reply, "but there's nae doot the lassie was fell fond o' me. Ou, a mere passin' fancy's ye micht say."

CHAPTER IX

DAVIT LUNAN'S POLITICAL REMINISCENCES

When an election-day comes round now, it takes me back to the time of 1832. I would be eight or ten year old at that time. James Strachan was at the door by five o'clock in the morning in his Sabbath clothes, by arrangement. We was to go up to the hill to see them building the bonfire. Moreover, there was word that Mr. Scrimgour was to be there tossing pennies, just like at a marriage. I was awakened before that by my mother at the pans and bowls. I have always associated elections since that time with jelly-making; for just as my mother would fill the cups and tankers and bowls with jelly to save cans, she was emptying the pots and pans to make way for the ale and porter. James and me was to help to carry it home from the square—him in the pitcher and me in a flagon, because I was silly for my age and not strong in the arms.

It was a very blowy morning, though the rain kept off, and what part of the bonfire had been built already was found scattered to the winds. Before we rose a great mass of folk was getting the barrels and things together again; but some of them was never recovered, and suspicion pointed to William Geddes, it being well known that William would not hesitate to carry off anything if unobserved. More by token Chirsty Lamby had seen him rolling home a barrowful of firewood early in the morning, her having risen to hold cold water in her mouth, being down with the toothache. When we got up to the hill everybody was making for the quarry, which being more sheltered was now thought to be a better place for the bonfire. The masons had struck work, it being a general holiday in the whole countryside. There was a great commotion of people, all fine dressed and mostly with glengarry bonnets; and me and James was well acquaint with them, though mostly weavers and the like and not my father's equal. Mr. Scrimgour was not there himself; but there was a small active body in his room as tossed the money for him fair enough; though not so liberally as was expected, being mostly ha'pence where pennies was looked for. Such was not my father's opinion, and him and a few others only had a vote. He considered it was a waste of money giving to them that had no vote and so taking out of other folks' mouths; but the little man said it kept everybody in good-humor and made Mr. Scrimgour popular. He was an extraordinary affable man and very spirity, running about to waste no time in walking, and gave me a shilling, saying to me to be a truthful boy and tell my father. He did not give James anything, him being an orphan, but clapped his head and said he was a fine boy.

The captain was to vote for the bill if he got in, the which he did. It was the captain was to give the ale and the porter in the square like a true gentleman. My father gave a kind of laugh when I let him see my shilling, and said he would keep care of it for me; and sorry I was I let him get it, me never seeing the face of it again to this day. Me and James was much annoyed with the women, especially Kitty Davie, always pushing in when there was tossing, and tearing the very ha'pence out of our hands: us not caring so much about the money, but humiliated to see women mixing up in politics. By the time the topmost barrel was on the bonfire there was a great smell of whiskey in the quarry, it being a confined place. My father had been against the bonfire being in the quarry, arguing that the wind on the hill would have carried off the smell of the whiskey; but Peter Tosh said they did not want the smell carried off; it would be agreeable to the masons for weeks to come. Except among the women, there was no fighting nor wrangling at the quarry, but all in fine spirits.

I misremember now whether it was Mr. Scrimgour or the captain that took the fancy to my father's pigs; but it was this day, at any rate, that the captain sent him the game-cock. Whichever one it was that fancied the litter of pigs, nothing would content him but to buy them, which he did at thirty shillings each, being the best bargain ever my father made. Nevertheless I'm thinking he was windier of the cock. The captain, who was a local man when not with his regiment, had the grandest collection of fighting-cocks in the county, and sometimes came into the town to try them against the town cocks. I mind well the large wicker cage in which they were conveyed from place to place, and never without the captain near at hand. My father had a cock that beat all the other town cocks at the cock-fight at our school, which was superintended by the elder of the kirk to see fair play; but the which died of its wounds the next day but one. This was a great grief to my father, it having been challenged to fight the captain's cock. Therefore it was very considerate of the captain to make my father a present of his bird; father, in compliment to him, changing its name from the "Deil" to the "Captain."

During the forenoon, and I think until well on in the day, James and me was busy with the pitcher and the flagon. The proceedings in the square, however, was not so well conducted as in the quarry, many of the folk there assembled showing a mean and grasping spirit. The captain had given orders that there was to be no stint of ale and porter, and neither there was; but much of it lost through hastiness. Great barrels was hurled into the middle of the square, where the country wives sat with their eggs and butter on market-day, and was quickly stove in with an axe or paving-stone or whatever came handy. Sometimes they would break into the barrel at different points; and then, when they tilted it up to get the ale out at one hole, it gushed out at the bottom till the square was flooded. My mother was fair disgusted when told by me and James of the waste of good liquor. It is gospel truth I speak when I say I mind well of seeing Singer Davie catching the porter in a pan as it ran down the sire, and when the pan was full to overflowing, putting his mouth to the stream and drinking till he was as full as the pan. Most of the men, however, stuck to the barrels, the drink running in the street being ale and porter mixed, and left it to the women and the young folk to do the carrying. Susy M'Queen brought as many pans as she could collect on a barrow, and was filling them all with porter, rejecting the ale; but indignation was aroused against her, and as fast as she filled the others emptied.

My father scorned to go to the square to drink ale and porter with the crowd, having the election on his mind and him to vote. Nevertheless he instructed me and James to keep up a brisk trade with the pans, and run back across the gardens in case we met dishonest folk in the streets who might drink the ale. Also, said my father, we was to let the excesses of our neighbors be a warning in sobriety to us; enough being as good as a feast, except when you can store it up for the winter. By and by my mother thought it was not safe me being in the streets with so many wild men about, and would have sent James himself, him being an orphan and hardier; but this I did not like, but, running out, did not come back for long enough. There is no doubt that the music was to blame for firing the men's blood, and the result most disgraceful fighting with no object in view. There was three fiddlers and two at the flute, most of them blind, but not the less dangerous on that account; and they kept the town in a ferment, even playing the country-folk home to the farms, followed by bands of towns-folk. They were a quarrelsome set, the ploughmen and others; and it was generally admitted in the town that their overbearing behavior was responsible for the fights. I mind them being driven out of the square, stones flying thick; also some stand-up fights with sticks, and others fair enough with fists. The worst fight I did not see. It took place in a field. At first it was only between two who had been miscalling one another; but there was many looking on, and when the town man was like getting the worst of it the others set to, and a most heathenish fray with no sense in it ensued. One man had his arm broken. I mind Hobart the bellman going about ringing his bell and telling all persons to get within doors; but little attention was paid to him, it being notorious that Snecky had had a fight earlier in the day himself.

When James was fighting in the field, according to his own account, I had the honor of dining with the electors who voted for the captain, him paying all expenses. It was a lucky accident my mother sending me to the town-house, where the dinner came off, to try to get my father home at a decent hour, me having a remarkable power over him when in liquor, but at no other time. They were very jolly, however, and insisted on my drinking the captain's health and eating more than was safe. My father got it next day from my mother for this; and so would I myself, but it was several days before I left my bed, completely knocked up as I was with the excitement and one thing or another. The bonfire, which was built to celebrate the election of Mr. Scrimgour, was set ablaze, though I did not see it, in honor of the election of the captain; it being thought a pity to lose it, as no doubt it would have been. That is about all I remember of the celebrated election of '32 when the Reform Bill was passed.

CHAPTER X

A VERY OLD FAMILY

They were a very old family with whom Snecky Hobart, the bellman, lodged. Their favorite dissipation, when their looms had come to rest, was a dander through the kirk-yard. They dressed for it: the three young ones in their rusty blacks; the patriarch in his old blue coat, velvet knee-breeches, and broad blue bonnet; and often of an evening I have met them moving from grave to grave. By this time the old man was nearly ninety, and the young ones averaged sixty. They read out the inscriptions on the tombstones in a solemn drone, and their father added his reminiscences. He never failed them. Since the beginning of the century he had not missed a funeral, and his children felt that he was a great example. Sire and sons returned from the cemetery invigorated for their daily labors. If one of them happened to start a dozen yards behind the others, he never thought of making up the distance. If his foot struck against a stone, he came to a dead stop; when he discovered that he had stopped, he set off again.

A high wall shut off this old family's house and garden, from the clatter of Thrums, a wall that gave Snecky some trouble before he went to live within it. I speak from personal knowledge. One spring morning, before the school-house was built, I was assisting the patriarch to divest the gaunt garden pump of its winter suit of straw. I was taking a drink, I remember, my palm over the mouth of the wooden spout and my mouth at the gimlet-hole above, when a leg appeared above the corner of the wall against which the hen-house was built. Two hands followed, clutching desperately at the uneven stones. Then the leg worked as if it were turning a grindstone, and next moment Snecky was sitting breathlessly on the dyke. From this to the hen-house, whose roof was of "divets," the descent was comparatively easy, and a slanting board allowed the daring bellman to slide thence to the ground. He had come on business, and having talked it over slowly with the old man he turned to depart. Though he was a genteel man, I heard him sigh heavily as, with the remark, "Ay, weel, I'll be movin' again," he began to rescale the wall. The patriarch, twisted round the pump, made no reply, so I ventured to suggest to the bellman that he might find the gate easier. "Is there a gate?" said Snecky, in surprise at the resources of civilization. I pointed it out to him, and he went his way chuckling. The old man told me that he had sometimes wondered at Snecky's mode of approach, but it had not struck him to say anything. Afterward, when the bellman took up his abode there, they discussed the matter heavily.

Hobart inherited both his bell and his nickname from his father, who was not a native of Thrums. He came from some distant part where the people speak of snecking the door, meaning shut it. In Thrums the word used is steek, and sneck seemed to the inhabitants so droll and ridiculous that Hobart got the name of Snecky. His son left Thrums at the age of ten for the distant farm of Tirl, and did not return until the old bellman's death, twenty years afterward; but the first remark he overheard on entering the kirk-wynd was a conjecture flung across the street by a gray-haired crone, that he would be "little Snecky come to bury auld Snecky."

The father had a reputation in his day for "crying" crimes he was suspected of having committed himself, but the Snecky I knew had too high a sense of his own importance for that. On great occasions, such as the loss of little Davy Dundas, or when a tattie roup had to be cried, he was even offensively inflated: but ordinary announcements, such as the approach of a flying stationer, the roup of a deceased weaver's loom, or the arrival in Thrums of a cart-load of fine "kebec" cheeses, he treated as the merest trifles. I see still the bent legs of the snuffy old man straightening to the tinkle of his bell, and the smirk with which he let the curious populace gather round him. In one hand he ostentatiously displayed the paper on which what he had to cry was written, but, like the minister, he scorned to "read." With the bell carefully tucked under his oxter he gave forth his news in a rasping voice that broke now and again into a squeal. Though Scotch in his unofficial conversation, he was believed to deliver himself on public occasions in the finest English. When trotting from place to place with his news he carried his bell by the tongue as cautiously as if it were a flagon of milk.

Snecky never allowed himself to degenerate into a mere machine. His proclamations were provided by those who employed him, but his soul was his own. Having cried a potato roup he would sometimes add a word of warning, such as, "I wudna advise ye, lads, to hae ony-thing to do wi' thae tatties; they're diseased." Once, just before thecattle market, he was sent round by a local laird to announce that any drover found taking the short cut to the hill through the grounds of Muckle Plowy would be prosecuted to the utmost limits of the law. The people were aghast. "Hoots, lads," Snecky said; "dinna fash yoursels. It's juist a haver o' the grieve's." One of Hobart's ways of striking terror into evil-doers was to announce, when crying a crime, that he himself knew perfectly well who the culprit was. "I see him brawly," he would say, "standing afore me, an' if he disna instantly mak retribution, I am determined this very day to mak a public example of him."

Before the time of the Burke and Hare murders Snecky's father was sent round Thrums to proclaim the startling news that a grave in the kirk-yard had been tampered with. The "resurrectionist" scare was at its height then, and the patriarch, who was one of the men in Thrums paid to watch new graves in the night-time, has often told the story. The town was in a ferment as the news spread, and there were fierce suspicious men among Hobart's hearers who already had the rifler of graves in their eye.

He was a man who worked for the farmers when they required an extra hand, and loafed about the square when they could do without him. No one had a good word for him, and lately he had been flush of money. That was sufficient. There was a rush of angry men through the "pend" that led to his habitation, and he was dragged, panting and terrified, to the kirk-yard before he understood what it all meant. To the grave they hurried him, and almost without a word handed him a spade. The whole town gathered round the spot—a sullen crowd, the women only breaking the silence with their sobs, and the children clinging to their gowns. The suspected resurrectionist understood what was wanted of him, and, flinging off his jacket, began to reopen the grave. Presently the spade struck upon wood, and by and by part of the coffin came in view. That was nothing, for the resurrectionists had a way of breaking the coffin at one end and drawing out the body with tongs. The digger knew this. He broke the boards with the spade and revealed an arm. The people convinced, he dropped the arm savagely, leaped out of the grave and went his way, leaving them to shovel back the earth themselves.

There was humor in the old family as well as in their lodger. I found this out slowly. They used to gather round their peat fire in the evening, after the poultry had gone to sleep on the kitchen rafters, and take off their neighbors. None of them ever laughed; but their neighbors did afford them subject for gossip, and the old man was very sarcastic over other people's old-fashioned ways. When one of the family wanted to go out he did it gradually. He would be sitting "into the fire" browning his corduroy trousers, and he would get up slowly. Then he gazed solemnly before him for a time, and after that, if you watched him narrowly, you would see that he was really moving to the door. Another member of the family took the vacant seat with the same precautions. Will'um, the eldest, has a gun, which customarily stands behind the old eight-day clock; and he takes it with him to the garden to shoot the blackbirds. Long before Will'um is ready to let fly, the blackbirds have gone away; and so the gun is never, never fired; but there is a determined look on Will'um's face when he returns from the garden.

In the stormy days of his youth the old man had been a "Black Nib." The Black Nibs were the persons who agitated against the French war; and the public feeling against them ran strong and deep. In Thrums the local Black Nibs were burned in effigy, and whenever they put their heads out of doors they risked being stoned. Even where the authorities were unprejudiced they were helpless to interfere; and as a rule they were as bitter against the Black Nibs as the populace themselves. Once the patriarch was running through the street with a score of the enemy at his heels, and the bailie, opening his window, shouted to them, "Stane the Black Nib oot o' the toon!"

When the patriarch was a young man he was a follower of pleasure. This is the one thing about him that his family have never been able to understand. A solemn stroll through the kirk-yard was not sufficient relaxation in those riotous times, after a hard day at the loom; and he rarely lost a chance of going to see a man hanged. There was a good deal of hanging in those days; and yet the authorities had an ugly way of reprieving condemned men on whom the sight-seers had been counting. An air of gloom would gather on my old friend's countenance when he told how he and his contemporaries in Thrums trudged every Saturday for six weeks to the county town, many miles distant, to witness the execution of some criminal in whom they had local interest, and who, after disappointing them again and again, was said to have been bought off by a friend. His crime had been stolen entrance into a house in Thrums by the chimney, with intent to rob; and though this old-fashioned family did not see it, not the least noticeable incident in the scrimmage that followed was the prudence of the canny housewife. When she saw the legs coming down the lum, she rushed to the kail-pot which was on the fire and put on the lid. She confessed that this was not done to prevent the visitor's scalding himself, but to save the broth.

The old man was repeated in his three sons. They told his stories precisely as he did himself, taking as long in the telling and making the points in exactly the same way. By and by they will come to think that they themselves were of those past times. Already the young ones look like contemporaries of their father.

CHAPTER XI

LITTLE RATHIE'S "BURAL"

Devout-under-difficulties would have been the name of Lang Tammas had he been of Covenanting times. So I thought one wintry afternoon, years before I went to the school-house, when he dropped in to ask the pleasure of my company to the farmer of Little Rathie's "bural." As a good Auld Licht, Tammas reserved his swallow-tail coat and "lum hat" (chimney-pot) for the kirk and funerals; but the coat would have flapped villanously, to Tammas' eternal ignominy, had he for one rash moment relaxed his hold of the bottom button, and it was only by walking sideways, as horses sometimes try to do, that the hat could be kept at the angle of decorum. Let it not he thought that Tammas had asked me to Little Rathie's funeral on his own responsibility. Burials were among the few events to break the monotony of an Auld Licht winter, and invitations were as much sought after as cards to my lady's dances in the south. This had been a fair average season for Tammas, though of his four burials one had been a bairn's—a mere bagatelle; but had it not been for the death of Little Rathie I would probably not have been out that year at all.

The small farm of Little Rathie lies two miles from Thrums, and Tammas and I trudged manfully through the snow, adding to our numbers as we went. The dress of none differed materially from the precentor's, and the general effect was of septuagenarians in each other's best clothes, though living in low-roofed houses had bent most of them before their time. By a rearrangement of garments, such as making Tammas change coat, hat, and trousers with Cragiebuckle, Silva McQueen, and Sam'l Wilkie respectively, a dexterous tailor might perhaps have supplied each with a "fit." The talk was chiefly of Little Rathie, and sometimes threatened to become animated, when another mourner would fall in and restore the more fitting gloom.

"Ay, ay," the new-comer would say, by way of responding to the sober salutation, "Ay, Johnny." Then there was silence, but for the "gluck" with which we lifted our feet from the slush.

"So Little Rathie's been ta'en awa'," Johnny would venture to say by and by.

"He's gone, Johnny; ay, man, he is so."

"Death must come to all," some one would waken up to murmur.

"Ay," Lang Tammas would reply, putting on the coping-stone, "in the morning we are strong and in the evening we are cut down."

"We are so, Tammas; ou ay, we are so; we're here the wan day an' gone the neist."

"Little Rathie wasna a crittur I took till; no, I canna say he was," said Bowie Haggart, so called because his legs described a parabola, "but be maks a vary creeditable corp [corpse]. I will say that for him. It's wonderfu' hoo death improves a body. Ye cudna hae said as Little Rathie was a weel-faured man when he was i' the flesh."

Bowie was the wright, and attended burials in his official capacity. He had the gift of words to an uncommon degree, and I do not forget his crushing blow at the reputation of the poet Burns, as delivered under the auspices of the Thrums Literary Society. "I am of opeenion," said Bowie, "that the works of Burns is of an immoral tendency. I have not read them myself, but such is my opeenion."

"He was a queer stock, Little Rathie, michty queer," said Tammas Haggart, Bowie's brother, who was a queer stock himself, but was not aware of it; "but, ou, I'm thinkin' the wife had something to do wi't. She was ill to manage, an' Little Rathie hadna the way o' the women. He hadna the knack o' managin' them's yo micht say—no, Little Rathie hadna the knack."

"They're kittle cattle, the women," said the farmer of Craigiebuckle—son of the Craigiebuckle mentioned elsewhere —a little gloomily. "I've often thocht maiterimony is no onlike the lucky bags th' auld wifies has at the muckly. There's prizes an' blanks baith inside, but, losh, ye're far frae sure what ye'll draw oot when ye put in yer han'."

"Ou, weel," said Tammas complacently, "there's truth in what ye say, but the women can be managed if ye have the knack."

"Some o' them," said Cragiebuckle woefully.

"Ye had yer wark wi' the wife yersel, Tammas, so ye had," observed Lang Tammas, unbending to suit his company.

"Ye're speakin' aboot the bit wife's bural," said Tammas Haggart, with a chuckle; "ay, ay, that brocht her to reason."

Without much pressure Haggart retold a story known to the majority of his hearers. He had not the "knack" of managing women apparently when he married, for he and his gypsy wife "agreed ill thegither" at first. Once Chirsty left him and took up her abode in a house just across the wynd. Instead of routing her out, Tammas, without taking any one into his confidence, determined to treat Chirsty as dead, and celebrate her decease in a "lyke wake"—a last wake. These wakes were very general in Thrums in the old days, though they had ceased to be common by the date of Little Rathie's death. For three days before the burial the friends and neighbors of the mourners were invited into the house to partake of food and drink by the side of the corpse. The dead lay on chairs covered with a white sheet. Dirges were sung and the deceased was extolled, but when night came the lights were extinguished and the corpse was left alone. On the morning of the funeral tables were spread with a white cloth outside the house, and food and drink were placed upon them. No neighbor could pass the tables without paying his respects to the dead; and even when the house was in a busy, narrow thoroughfare, this part of the ceremony was never omitted. Tammas did not give Chirsty a wake inside the house; but one Friday morning—it was market-day, and the square was consequently full—it went through the town that the tables were spread before his door. Young and old collected, wandering round the house, and Tammas stood at the tables in his blacks inviting every one to eat and drink. He was pressed to tell what it meant; but nothing could be got from him except that his wife was dead. At times he pressed his hands to his heart, and then he would make wry faces, trying hard to cry. Chirsty watched from a window across the street, until she perhaps began to fear that she really was dead. Unable to stand it any longer, she rushed out into her husband's arms, and shortly afterward she could have been seen dismantling the tables.

"She's gone this fower year," Tammas said, when he had finished his story, "but up to the end I had no more trouble wi' Chirsty. No, I had the knack o' her.'

"I've heard tell, though," said the sceptical Craigiebuckle, "as Chirsty only cam back to ye because she cudna bear to see the fowk makkin' sae free wi' the whiskey."

"I mind hoo she bottled it up at ance and drove the laddies awa'," said Bowie, "an' I hae seen her after that, Tammas, giein' ye up yer fut an' you no sayin' a word."

"Ou, ay," said the wife-tamer, in the tone of a man who could afford to be generous in trifles, "women maun talk, an' a man hasna aye time to conterdick them, but frae that day I had the knack o' Chirsty."

"Donal Elshioner's was a vary seemilar case," broke in Snecky Hobart shrilly. "Maist o' ye'll mind 'at Donal was michty plagueit wi' a drucken wife. Ay, weel, wan day Bowie's man was carryin' a coffin past Donal's door, and Donal an' the wife was there. Says Donal, 'Put doon yer coffin, my man, an' tell's wha it's for.' The laddie rests the coffin on its end, an' says he, 'It's for Davie Fairbrother's guid-wife.' 'Ay, then,' says Donal, 'tak it awa', tak it awa' to Davie, an' tell 'im as ye kin a man wi' a wife 'at wid be glad to neifer [exchange] wi' him.' Man, that terrified Donal's wife; it did so."

As we delved up the twisting road between two fields that leads to the farm of Little Rathie, the talk became less general, and another mourner who joined us there was told that the farmer was gone.

"We must all fade as a leaf," said Lang Tammas.

"So we maun, so we maun," admitted the new-comer. "They say," he added, solemnly, "as Little Rathie has left a full teapot."

The reference was to the safe in which the old people in the district stored their gains.

"He was thrifty," said Tammas Haggart, "an' shrewd, too, was Little Rathie. I mind Mr. Dishart admonishin' him for no attendin' a special weather service i' the kirk, when Finny an' Lintool, the twa adjoinin' farmers, baith attendit. 'Ou,' says Little Rathie, 'I thocht to mysel, thinks I, if they get rain for prayin' for't on Finny an' Lintool, we're bound to get the benefit o't on Little Rathie.'"

"Tod," said Snecky, "there's some sense in that; an' what says the minister?"

"I d'na kin what he said," admitted Haggart; "but he took Little Rathie up to the manse, an' if ever I saw a man lookin' sma', it was Little Rathie when he cam oot."

The deceased had left behind him a daughter (herself now known as Little Rathie), quite capable of attending to the ramshackle "but and ben;" and I remember how she nipped off Tammas' consolations to go out and feed the hens. To the number of about twenty we assembled round the end of the house to escape the bitter wind, and here I lost the precentor, who, as an Auld Licht elder, joined the chief mourners inside. The post of distinction at a funeral is near the coffin; but it is not given to every one to be a relative of the deceased, and there is always much competition and genteelly concealed disappointment over the few open vacancies. The window of the room was decently veiled, but the mourners outside knew what was happening within, and that it was not all prayer, neither mourning. A few of the more reverent uncovered their heads at intervals; but it would be idle to deny that there was a feeling that Little Rathie's daughter was favoring Tammas and others somewhat invidiously. Indeed, Robbie Gibruth did not scruple to remark that she had made "an inauspeecious beginning." Tammas Haggart, who was melancholy when not sarcastic, though he brightened up wonderfully at funerals, reminded Robbie that disappointment is the lot of man on his earthly pilgrimage; but Haggart knew who were to be invited back after the burial to the farm, and was inclined, to make much of his position. The secret would doubtless have been wormed from him had not public attention been directed into another channel. A prayer was certainly being offered up inside; but the voice was not the voice of the minister.

Lang Tammas told me afterward that it had seemed at one time "vary queistionable" whether Little Rathie would be buried that day at all. The incomprehensible absence of Mr. Dishart (afterward satisfactorily explained) had raised the unexpected question of the legality of a burial in a case where the minister had not prayed over the "corp." There had even been an indulgence in hot words, and the Reverend Alexander

Kewans, a "stickit minister," but not of the Auld Licht persuasion, had withdrawn in dudgeon on hearing Tammas asked to conduct the ceremony instead of himself. But, great as Tammas was on religious questions, a pillar of the Auld Licht kirk, the Shorter Catechism at his finger-ends, a sad want of words at the very time when he needed them most incapacitated him for prayer in public, and it was providential that Bowie proved himself a man of parts. But Tammas tells me that the wright grossly abused his position, by praying at such length that Craigiebuckle fell asleep, and the mistress had to rise and hang the pot on the fire higher up the joist, lest its contents should burn before the return from the funeral. Loury grew the sky, and more and more anxious the face of Little Rathie's daughter, and still Bowie prayed on. Had it not been for the impatience of the precentor and the grumbling of the mourners outside, there is no saying when the remains would have been lifted through the "bole," or little window.

Hearses had hardly come in at this time, and the coffin was carried by the mourners on long stakes. The straggling procession of pedestrians behind wound its slow way in the waning light to the kirk-yard, showing startlingly black against the dazzling snow; and it was not until the earth rattled on the coffin-lid that Little Rathie's nearest male relative seemed to remember his last mournful duty to the dead. Sidling up to the favored mourners, he remarked casually and in the most emotionless tone he could assume; "They're expec'in' ye to stap doon the length o' Little Rathie noo. Aye, aye, he's gone. Na, na, nae refoosal, Da-avit; ye was aye a guid friend till him, an' it's onything a body can do for him noo."

Though the uninvited slunk away sorrowfully, the entertainment provided at Auld Licht houses of mourning was characteristic of a stern and sober sect. They got to eat and to drink to the extent, as a rule, of a "lippy" of short bread and a "brew" of toddy; but open Bibles lay on the table, and the eyes of each were on his neighbors to catch them transgressing, and offer up a prayer for them on the spot. Ay me! there is no Bowie nowadays to fill an absent minister's shoes.

CHAPTER XII

A LITERARY CLUB

The ministers in the town did not hold with literature. When the most notorious of the clubs met in the town-house under the presidentship of Gravia Ogilvy, who was no better than a poacher, and was troubled in his mind because writers called Pope a poet, there was frequently a wrangle over the question, "Is literature necessarily immoral?" It was a fighting club, and on Friday nights the few respectable, God-fearing members dandered to the town-house, as if merely curious to have another look at the building. If Lang Tammas, who was dead against letters, was in sight they wandered off, but when there were no spies abroad they slunk up the stair. The attendance was greatest on dark nights, though Gavin himself and some other characters would have marched straight to the meeting in broad daylight. Tammas Haggart, who did not think much of Milton's devil, had married a gypsy woman for an experiment, and the Coat of Many Colors did not know where his wife was. As a rule, however, the members were wild bachelors. When they married they had to settle down.

Gavin's essay on Will'um Pitt, the Father of the Taxes, led to the club's being bundled out of the town-house, where people said it should never have been allowed to meet. There was a terrible towse when Tammas Haggart then disclosed the secret of Mr. Byars' supposed approval of the club. Mr. Byars was the Auld Licht minister whom Mr. Dishart succeeded, and it was well known that he had advised the authorities to grant the use of the little town-house to the club on Friday evenings. As he solemnly warned his congregation against attending the meetings, the position he had taken up created talk, and Lang Tammas called at the manse with Sanders Whamond to remonstrate. The minister, however, harangued them on their sinfulness in daring to question the like of him, and they had to retire vanquished though dissatisfied. Then came the disclosures of Tammas Haggart, who was never properly secured by the Auld Lichts until Mr. Dishart took him in hand. It was Tammas who wrote anonymous letters to Mr. Byars about the scarlet woman, and, strange to say, this led to the club's being allowed to meet in the town-house. The minister, after many days, discovered who his correspondent was, and succeeded in inveigling the stone-breaker to the manse. There, with the door snibbed, he opened out on Tammas, who, after his usual manner when hard pressed, pretended to be deaf. This sudden fit of deafness so exasperated the minister that he flung a book at Tammas. The scene that followed was one that few Auld Licht manses can have witnessed. According to Tammas, the book had hardly reached the floor when the minister turned white. Tammas picked up the missile. It was a Bible. The two men looked at each other. Beneath the window Mr. Byars' children were prattling. His wife was moving about in the next room, little thinking what had happened. The minister held out his hand for the Bible, but Tammas shook his head, and then Mr. Byars shrank into a chair. Finally, it was arranged that if Tammas kept the affair to himself the minister would say a good word to the bailie about the literary club. After that the stone-breaker used to go from house to house, twisting his mouth to the side and remarking that he could tell such a tale of Mr. Byars as would lead to a split in the kirk. When the town-house was locked on the club Tammas spoke out, but though the scandal ran from door to door, as I have seen a pig in a fluster do, the minister did not lose his place. Tammas preserved the Bible, and showed it complacently to visitors as the present he got from Mr. Byars. The minister knew this, and it turned his temper sour. Tammas' proud moments, after that, were when he passed the minister.

Driven from the town-house, literature found a table with forms round it in a tavern hard by, where the club, lopped of its most respectable members, kept the blinds down and talked openly of Shakespeare. It was a low-roofed room, with pieces of lime hanging from the ceiling and peeling walls. The floor had a slope that tended to fling the debater forward, and its boards, lying loose on an uneven foundation, rose and looked at you as you crossed the room. In winter, when the meetings were held regularly every fortnight, a fire of peat, sod, and dross lit up the curious company who sat round the table shaking their heads over Shelley's mysticism, or requiring to be called to order because they would not wait their turn to deny an essayist's assertion, that Berkeley's style was superior to David Hume's. Davit Hume, they said, and Watty Scott. Burns was simply referred to as Rob or Robbie.

There was little drinking at these meetings, for the members knew what they were talking about, and your mind had to gallop to keep up with the flow of reasoning. Thrums is rather a remarkable town. There are scores and scores of houses in it that have sent their sons to college (by what a struggle!), some to make their way to the front in their professions, and others, perhaps, despite their broadcloth, never to be a patch on their parents. In that literary club there were men of a reading so wide and catholic that it might put some graduates of the universities to shame, and of an intellect so keen that had it not had a crook in it their fame would have crossed the county. Most of them had but a threadbare existence, for you weave slowly with a Wordsworth open before you, and some were strange Bohemians (which does not do in Thrums), yet others wandered into the world and compelled it to recognize them. There is a London barrister whose father belonged to the club. Not many years ago a man died on the staff of the *Times*, who, when he was a weaver near Thrums, was one of the club's prominent members. He taught himself shorthand by the light of a cruizey, and got a post on a Perth paper, afterward on the *Scotsman* and the *Witness*, and finally on the *Times*. Several other men of his type had a history worth reading, but it is not for me to write. Yet I may say that there is still at least one of the original members of the club left behind in Thrums to whom some of the literary dandies might lift their hats.

Gavin Ogilvy I only knew as a weaver and a poacher: a lank, long-armed man, much bent from crouching in ditches whence he watched his snares. To the young he was a romantic figure, because they saw him frequently in the fields with his call-birds tempting siskins, yellow yites, and Unties to twigs which he had previously smeared with lime. He made the lime from the tough roots of holly; sometimes from linseed, oil, which is boiled until thick, when it is taken out of the pot and drawn and stretched with the hands like elastic. Gavin was also a famous hare-snarer at a time when the ploughman looked upon this form of poaching as his perquisite. The snare was of wire, so constructed that the hare entangled itself the more when trying to escape, and it was placed across the little roads through the fields to which hares confine themselves, with a heavy stone attached to it by a string. Once Gavin caught a toad (fox) instead of a hare, and did not discover his mistake until it had him by the teeth. He was not able to weave for two months. The grouse-netting was more lucrative and more exciting, and women engaged in it with their husbands. It is told of Gavin that he was on one occasion chased by a game-keeper over moor and hill for twenty miles, and that by and by when the one sank down exhausted so did the other. They would sit fifty yards apart, glaring at each other. The poacher eventually escaped. This, curious as it may seem, is the man whose eloquence at the club has not been forgotten in fifty years. "Thus did he stand," I have been told recently, "exclaiming in language sublime that the soul shall bloom in immortal youth through the ruin and wrack of time."

Another member read to the club an account of his journey to Lochnagar, which was afterward published in *Chambers's Journal.* He was celebrated for his descriptions of scenery, and was not the only member of the club whose essays got into print. More memorable perhaps was an itinerant match-seller known to Thrums and the surrounding towns as the literary spunk-seller. He was a wizened, shivering old man, often barefooted, wearing at the best a thin, ragged coat that had been black but was green-brown with age, and he made his spunks as well as sold them. He brought Bacon and Adam Smith into Thrums, and he loved to recite long screeds from Spenser, with a running commentary on the versification and the luxuriance of the diction. Of Jamie's death I do not care to write. He went without many a dinner in order to buy a book.

The Coat of Many Colors and Silva Robbie were two street preachers who gave the Thrums ministers some work. They occasionally appeared at the club. The Coat of Many Colors was so called because he wore a garment consisting of patches of cloth of various colors sewed together. It hung down to his heels. He may have been cracked rather than inspired, but he was a power in the square where he preached, the women declaring that he was gifted by God. An awe filled even the men when he admonished them for using strong language, for at such a time he would remind them of the woe which fell upon Tibbie Mason. Tibbie had been notorious in her day for evil-speaking, especially for her free use of the word handless, which she flung a hundred times in a week at her man, and even at her old mother. Her punishment was to have a son born without hands. The Coat of Many Colors also told of the liar who exclaimed, "If this is not gospel true may I stand here forever," and who is standing on that spot still, only nobody knows where it is. George Wishart was the Coat's hero, and often he has told in the square how Wishart saved Dundee. It was the time when the plague lay over Scotland, and in Dundee they saw it approaching from the West in the form of a great black cloud. They fell on their knees and prayed, crying to the cloud to pass them by, and while they prayed it came nearer. Then they looked around for the most holy man among them, to intervene with God on their behalf. All eyes turned to George Wishart, and he stood up, stretching his arms to the cloud, and prayed, and it rolled back. Thus Dundee was saved from the plague, but when Wishart ended his prayer he was alone, for the people had all returned to their homes. Less of a genuine man than the Coat of Many Colors was Silva Robbie, who had horrid fits of laughing in the middle of his prayers, and even fell in a paroxysm of laughter from the chair on which he stood. In the club he said, things not to be borne, though logical up to a certain point.

Tammas Haggart was the most sarcastic member of the club, being celebrated for his sarcasm far and wide. It was a remarkable thing about him, often spoken of, that if you went to Tammas with a stranger and asked him to say a sarcastic thing that the man might take away as a specimen, he could not do it. "Na, na," Tammas would say, after a few trials, referring to sarcasm, "she's no a crittur to force. Ye maun lat her tak her ain time. Sometimes she's dry like the pump, an' syne, again, oot she comes in a gush." The most sarcastic thing the stone-breaker ever said was frequently marvelled over in Thrums, both before and behind his face, but unfortunately no one could ever remember what it was. The subject, however, was Cha Tamson's potato pit. There is little doubt that it was a fit of sarcasm that induced Tammas to marry a gypsy lassie. Mr. Byars would not join them, so Tammas had himself married by Jimmy Pawse, the gay little gypsy king, and after that the minister remarried them. The marriage over the tongs is a thing to scandalize any well-brought-up person, for before he joined the couple's hands Jimmy jumped about in a startling way, uttering wild gibberish, and after the ceremony was over there was rough work, with incantations and blowing on pipes. Tammas always held that this marriage turned out better than he had expected, though he had his trials like other married men. Among them was Chirsty's way of climbing on to the dresser to get at the higher part of the plate-rack. One evening I called in to have a smoke with the stone-breaker, and while we were talking Chirsty climbed the dresser. The next moment she was on the floor on her back, wailing, but Tammas smoked on imperturbably. "Do you not see what has happened, man?" I cried. "Ou," said Tammas, "she's aye fa'in aff the dresser."

Of the school-masters who were at times members of the club, Mr. Dickie was the ripest scholar, but my predecessor at the schoolhouse had a way of sneering at him that was as good as sarcasm. When they were on their legs at the same time, asking each other passionately to be calm, and rolling out lines from Homer that made the inn-keeper look fearfully to the fastenings of the door, their heads very nearly came together, although the table was between them. The old dominie had an advantage in being the shorter man, for he could hammer on the table as he spoke, while gaunt Mr. Dickie had to stoop to it. Mr. McRittie's arguments were a series of nails that he knocked into the table, and he did it in a workmanlike manner. Mr. Dickie, though he kept firm on his feet, swayed his body until by and by his head was rotating in a large circle. The mathematical figure he made was a cone revolving on its apex. Gavin's reinstalment in the chair year after year was made by the disappointed dominie the subject of some tart verses which be called an epode, but Gavin crushed him when they were read before the club. "Satire," he said, "is a legitimate weapon, used with michty effect by Swift, Sammy Butler, and others, and I dount object to being made the subject of creeticism. It has often been called a t'nife [knife], but them as is not used to t'nives cuts their hands, and ye'll a' observe that Mr. McRittie's fingers is bleedin'." All eyes were turned upon the dominie's hand, and though he pocketed it smartly several members had seen the blood. The dominie was a rare visitor at the club after that, though he outlived poor Mr. Dickie by many years. Mr. Dickie was a teacher in Tilliedrum, but he was ruined by drink. He wandered from town to town, reciting Greek and Latin poetry to any one who would give him a dram, and sometimes he wept and moaned aloud in the street, crying, "Poor Mr. Dickie! poor Mr. Dickie!"

The leading poet in a club of poets was Dite Walls, who kept a school when there were scholars and weaved when there were none. He had a song that was published in a halfpenny leaflet about the famous lawsuit instituted by the fanner of Teuchbusses against the Laird of Drumlee. The laird was alleged to have taken from the land of Teuchbusses sufficient broom to make a besom thereof, and I am not certain that the case is settled to this day. It was Dite, or another member of the club, who wrote "The Wife o' Deeside," of all the songs of the period the one that had the greatest vogue in the county at a time when Lord Jeffrey was cursed at every fireside in Thrums. The wife of Deeside was tried for the murder of her servant, who had infatuated the young laird, and had it not been that Jeffrey defended her she would, in the words of the song, have "hung like a troot." It is not easy now to conceive the rage against Jeffrey when the woman was acquitted. The song was sung and recited in the streets, at the smiddy, in bothies, and by firesides, to the shaking of fists and the grinding of teeth. It began:

"Ye'll a' hae hear tell o' the wife o' Deeside,
Ye'll a' hae hear tell o' the wife o' Deeside,
She poisoned her maid for to keep up her pride,
Ye'll a' hae hear tell o' the wife o' Deeside."

Before the excitement had abated, Jeffrey was in Tilliedrum for electioneering purposes, and he was mobbed in the streets. Angry crowds pressed close to howl "Wife o' Deeside!" at him. A contingent from Thrums was there, and it was long afterward told of Sam'l Todd, by himself, that he hit Jeffrey on the back of the head with a clod of earth.

Johnny McQuhatty, a brother of the T'nowhead farmer, was the one taciturn member of the club, and you had only to look at him to know that he had a secret. He was a great genius at the hand-loom, and invented a loom for the weaving of linen such as has not been seen before or since. In the day-time he kept guard over his "shop," into which no one was allowed to enter, and the fame of his loom was so great that he had to watch over it with a gun. At night he weaved, and when the result at last pleased him he made the linen into shirts, all of which he stitched together with his own hands, even to the button-holes. He sent one shirt to the Queen, and another to the Duchess of Athole, mentioning a very large price for them, which he got. Then he destroyed his wonderful loom, and how it was made no one will ever know. Johnny only took to literature after he had made his name, and he seldom spoke at the club except when ghosts and the like were the subject of debate, as they tended to be when the farmer of Mucklo Haws could get in a word. Mucklo Haws was fascinated by Johnny's sneers at superstition, and sometimes on dark nights the inventor had to make his courage good by seeing the farmer past the doulie yates (ghost gates), which Muckle Haws had to go perilously near on his way home. Johnny was a small man, but it was the burly farmer who shook at sight of the gates standing out white in the night. White gates have an evil name still, and Muckle Haws was full of horrors as he drew near them, clinging to Johnny's arm. It was on such a night, he would remember, that he saw the White Lady go through the gates greeting sorely, with a dead bairn in her arms, while water kelpie laughed and splashed in the pools and the witches danced in a ring round Broken Buss. That very night twelve months ago the packman was murdered at Broken Buss, and Easie Pettie hanged herself on the stump of a tree. Last night there were ugly sounds from the quarry of Croup, where the bairn lies buried, and it's not mous (canny) to be out at such a time. The farmer had seen spectre maidens walking round the ruined castle of Darg, and the castle all lit up with flaring torches, and dead knights and ladies sitting in the halls at the wine-cup, and the devil himself flapping his wings on the ramparts.

When the debates were political, two members with the gift of song fired the blood with their own poems about taxation and the depopulation of the Highlands, and by selling these songs from door to door they made their livelihood.

Books and pamphlets were brought into the town by the flying stationers, as they were called, who visited the square periodically carrying their wares on their backs, except at the Muckly, when they had their stall and even sold books by auction. The flying stationer best known to Thrums was Sandersy Riaca, who was stricken from head to foot with the palsy, and could only speak with a quaver in consequence. Sandersy brought to the members of the club all the great books he could get second-hand, but his stock in trade was Thrummy Cap and Akenstaff, the Fishwives of Buckhaven, the Devil upon Two Sticks, Gilderoy, Sir James the Rose, the Brownie of Badenoch, the Ghaist of Firenden, and the like. It was from Sandersy that Tammas Haggart bought his copy of Shakespeare, whom Mr. Dishart could never abide. Tammas kept what he had done from his wife, but Chirsty saw a deterioration setting in and told the minister of her suspicions. Mr. Dishart was newly placed at the time and very vigorous, and the way he shook the truth out of Tammas was grand. The minister pulled Tammas the one way and Gavin pulled him the other, but Mr. Dishart was not the man to be beaten, and he landed Tammas in the Auld Licht kirk before the year was out. Chirsty buried Shakespeare in the yard.

ABOUT THE AUTHOR

Sir James Matthew Barrie, 1st Baronet, OM (9 May 1860 – 19 June 1937), more commonly known as J. M. Barrie, was a Scottish novelist and dramatist. Most people remember him for inventing the character of Peter Pan, whom he based on his friends, the Llewelyn Davies boys.

Born in Kirriemuir, Angus, the second-youngest of ten children, Barrie received his formal education at the Glasgow Academy and the University of Edinburgh. He became a journalist in Nottingham, then London, and turned to writing novels and subsequently plays.

Made a baronet in 1913, Barrie lies buried at Kirriemuir next to his parents, sister, and elder brother David, who had died in a skating accident just before his 14th birthday.

Barrie often wrote dialogue in Scots. His Thrums novels were hugely successful when they were published starting with Auld Licht Idylls (1888). Next came A Window in Thrums (1889), and The Little Minister (1891). His two 'Tommy' novels Sentimental Tommy and Tommy and Grizel came in 1896 and 1902 and dealt with themes much more explicitly related to what would become Peter Pan. The first appearance of Pan came in The Little White Bird (1901).

Friedrich Kerst
Friedrich Nietzsche
Fyodor Dostoyevsky
G.A. Henty
G.K. Chesterton
Gabrielle E. Jackson
Garrett P. Serviss
Gaston Leroux
George A. Warren
George Ade
Geroge Bernard Shaw
George Cary Eggleston
George Durston
George Ebers
George Eliot
George Gissing
George MacDonald
George Meredith
George Orwell
George Sylvester Viereck
George Tucker
George W. Cable
George Wharton James
Gertrude Atherton
Gordon Casserly
Grace E. King
Grace Gallatin
Grace Greenwood
Grant Allen
Guillermo A. Sherwell
Gulielma Zollinger
Gustav Flaubert
H. A. Cody
H. B. Irving
H.C. Bailey
H. G. Wells
H. H. Munro
H. Irving Hancock
H. R. Naylor
H. Rider Haggard
H. W. C. Davis
Haldeman Julius
Hall Caine
Hamilton Wright Mabie
Hans Christian Andersen
Harold Avery
Harold McGrath
Harriet Beecher Stowe
Harry Castlemon
Harry Coghill
Harry Houidini
Hayden Carruth
Helent Hunt Jackson
Helen Nicolay
Hendrik Conscience
Hendy David Thoreau
Henri Barbusse
Henrik Ibsen
Henry Adams
Henry Ford
Henry Frost
Henry James
Henry Jones Ford
Henry Seton Merriman
Henry W Longfellow
Herbert A. Giles
Herbert Carter
Herbert N. Casson
Herman Hesse
Hildegard G. Frey
Homer
Honore De Balzac
Horace B. Day
Horace Walpole
Horatio Alger Jr.
Howard Pyle
Howard R. Garis
Hugh Lofting
Hugh Walpole
Humphry Ward
Ian Maclaren
Inez Haynes Gillmore
Irving Bacheller
Isabel Cecilia Williams
Isabel Hornibrook
Israel Abrahams
Ivan Turgenev
J.G.Austin
J. Henri Fabre
J. M. Barrie
J. M. Walsh
J. Macdonald Oxley
J. R. Miller
J. S. Fletcher
J. S. Knowles
J. Storer Clouston
J. W. Duffield
Jack London
Jacob Abbott
James Allen
James Andrews
James Baldwin
James Branch Cabell
James DeMille
James Joyce
James Lane Allen
James Lane Allen
James Oliver Curwood
James Oppenheim
James Otis
James R. Driscoll
Jane Abbott
Jane Austen
Jane L. Stewart
Janet Aldridge
Jens Peter Jacobsen
Jerome K. Jerome
Jessie Graham Flower
John Buchan
John Burroughs
John Cournos
John F. Kennedy
John Gay
John Glasworthy
John Habberton
John Joy Bell
John Kendrick Bangs
John Milton
John Philip Sousa
John Taintor Foote
Jonas Lauritz Idemil Lie
Jonathan Swift
Joseph A. Altsheler
Joseph Carey
Joseph Conrad
Joseph E. Badger Jr
Joseph Hergesheimer
Joseph Jacobs
Jules Vernes
Julian Hawthrone
Julie A Lippmann
Justin Huntly McCarthy
Kakuzo Okakura
Karle Wilson Baker
Kate Chopin
Kenneth Grahame
Kenneth McGaffey
Kate Langley Bosher
Kate Langley Bosher
Katherine Cecil Thurston
Katherine Stokes
L. A. Abbot
L. T. Meade

L. Frank Baum
Latta Griswold
Laura Dent Crane
Laura Lee Hope
Laurence Housman
Lawrence Beasley
Leo Tolstoy
Leonid Andreyev
Lewis Carroll
Lewis Sperry Chafer
Lilian Bell
Lloyd Osbourne
Louis Hughes
Louis Joseph Vance
Louis Tracy
Louisa May Alcott
Lucy Fitch Perkins
Lucy Maud Montgomery
Luther Benson
Lydia Miller Middleton
Lyndon Orr
M. Corvus
M. H. Adams
Margaret E. Sangster
Margret Howth
Margaret Vandercook
Margaret W. Hungerford
Margret Penrose
Maria Edgeworth
Maria Thompson Daviess
Mariano Azuela
Marion Polk Angellotti
Mark Overton
Mark Twain
Mary Austin
Mary Catherine Crowley
Mary Cole
Mary Hastings Bradley
Mary Roberts Rinehart
Mary Rowlandson
M. Wollstonecraft Shelley
Maud Lindsay
Max Beerbohm
Myra Kelly
Nathaniel Hawthrone
Nicolo Machiavelli
O. F. Walton
Oscar Wilde
Owen Johnson
P.G. Wodehouse
Paul and Mabel Thorne
Paul G. Tomlinson
Paul Severing
Percy Brebner
Percy Keese Fitzhugh
Peter B. Kyne
Plato
Quincy Allen
R. Derby Holmes
R. L. Stevenson
R. S. Ball
Rabindranath Tagore
Rahul Alvares
Ralph Bonehill
Ralph Henry Barbour
Ralph Victor
Ralph Waldo Emmerson
Rene Descartes
Ray Cummings
Rex Beach
Rex E. Beach
Richard Harding Davis
Richard Jefferies
Richard Le Gallienne
Robert Barr
Robert Frost
Robert Gordon Anderson
Robert L. Drake
Robert Lansing
Robert Lynd
Robert Michael Ballantyne
Robert W. Chambers
Rosa Nouchette Carey
Rudyard Kipling
Saint Augustine
Samuel B. Allison
Samuel Hopkins Adams
Sarah Bernhardt
Sarah C. Hallowell
Selma Lagerlof
Sherwood Anderson
Sigmund Freud
Standish O'Grady
Stanley Weyman
Stella Benson
Stella M. Francis
Stephen Crane
Stewart Edward White
Stijn Streuvels
Swami Abhedananda
Swami Parmananda
T. S. Ackland
T. S. Arthur
The Princess Der Ling
Thomas A. Janvier
Thomas A Kempis
Thomas Anderton
Thomas Bailey Aldrich
Thomas Bulfinch
Thomas De Quincey
Thomas Dixon
Thomas H. Huxley
Thomas Hardy
Thomas More
Thornton W. Burgess
U. S. Grant
Upton Sinclair
Valentine Williams
Various Authors
Vaughan Kester
Victor Appleton
Victor G. Durham
Victoria Cross
Virginia Woolf
Wadsworth Camp
Walter Camp
Walter Scott
Washington Irving
Wilbur Lawton
Wilkie Collins
Willa Cather
Willard F. Baker
William Dean Howells
William le Queux
W. Makepeace Thackeray
William W. Walter
William Shakespeare
Winston Churchill
Yei Theodora Ozaki
Yogi Ramacharaka
Young E. Allison
Zane Grey

www.ingramcontent.com/pod-product-compliance
Lightning Source LLC
Chambersburg PA
CBHW020548310726
48979CB00008B/1130/J
* 9 7 8 1 4 2 1 8 3 8 6 4 9 *